Praise for The Supporting Cast of the Bible

"Gina Hens-Piazza's work is always engaging and insightful. This book is no exception. Employing a diverse range of critical methods, Hens-Piazza focuses on characters in the Bible that usually go unnoticed or ignored by readers, not least by biblical scholars. Using stories from the book of Kings as examples, she shows how this neglect not only robs the stories of their richness but also carries ethical implications for modern audiences. The clear writing style makes for an easy read, and the observations are eye-opening and thought-provoking." —**Steven L. McKenzie**, Rhodes College

"Hens-Piazza over the years has distinguished herself as a champion for the so-called minor characters whose role in the biblical narratives are not so minor. In her new book, she continues this labor of love and offers a fascinating account of the supporting cast in the Hebrew Bible as illustrated by her careful and creative literary readings of selected narratives from 2 Kings. Drawing our attention to the characters who play complementary roles or bit parts, make cameo appearances, or are merely implied in the text, Hens-Piazza insists that every character deserves a hearing. By being mindful of the role that gender and class play in determining who counts and who does not, Hens-Piazza reverts our gaze to our own world, away from who and what society deems to be most powerful and most worthy of attention, to those individuals whose contributions to society are seldom recognized but are equally, and in some cases, perhaps even more important." —**L. Juliana Claassens**, Stellenbosch University

The Supporting Cast of the Bible

The Supporting Cast of the Bible

Reading on Behalf of the Multitude

Gina Hens-Piazza

LEXINGTON BOOKS/FORTRESS ACADEMIC
Lanham • Boulder • New York • London

Published by Lexington Books/Fortress Academic
Lexington Books is an imprint of The Rowman & Littlefield Publishing Group, Inc.
4501 Forbes Boulevard, Suite 200, Lanham, Maryland 20706
www.rowman.com

6 Tinworth Street, London SE11 5AL

Copyright © 2020 by The Rowman & Littlefield Publishing Group, Inc.

All rights reserved. No part of this book may be reproduced in any form or by any electronic or mechanical means, including information storage and retrieval systems, without written permission from the publisher, except by a reviewer who may quote passages in a review.

British Library Cataloguing in Publication Information Available

Library of Congress Cataloging-in-Publication Data Available

ISBN 9781978706934 (cloth)
ISBN 9781978706958 (pbk)
ISBN 9781978706941 (electronic)

For my son, Gabriel,
who always teaches me perseverance and a steadfastness of spirit.

Contents

Acknowledgments		ix
1	Making a Case for the Supporting Cast	1
2	Foregrounding the Backstory	13
3	Violence in Disguise: A Study of a Complementary Character in 2 Kings 6:23–31	33
4	Unsung Courage and Fidelity: A Study of Bit-Part Characters in 2 Kings 5:1–19	47
5	Vessels of Hope versus Hallmarks of Despair: A Study of Cameo Appearance Characters in 2 Kings 4:1–7	65
6	Lost in the Telling but Still Present: A Study of Implied Characters in 1 Kings 9:10–14	79
Conclusion		93
Bibliography		99
Scripture Index		105
Subject Index		109
About the Author		117

Acknowledgments

Some years ago, I wrote a commentary on 1 and 2 Kings. During three years of steady research and writing, I was struck daily by how many nameless individual characters and their stories I was reading past in order to interpret the grand tale of the protagonist, most often a king. An invitation to give the Distinguished Faculty Lecture at the Graduate Theological Union during that time period provided the occasion to test out whether it was possible to fix attention upon a few from this multitude of anonymous biblical characters. That overture, "Supporting Cast vs. Supporting Caste: The Major Importance of Minor Biblical Characters," proved both provocative and fruitful. With the subsequent encouragement of my colleagues and graduate students, the individual studies that eventually composed this book gradually began to take shape.

I want to thank my colleagues at the Jesuit School of Theology for the opportunity to present drafts of some of the chapters at our monthly faculty colloquium. Their careful reading of early essays and comments helped to hone and sharpen the thesis of the overall project. In addition, the faculties at the Ateneo de Manila; L'Institut de Théologie de la Compagnie de Jésus–Abidjan, Cote d'Ivoire; and at Hekima College, Nairobi, Kenya, all hosted forums for the presentation of some of this work while in process. For the reception, hospitality, and comments of these international colleagues on this project, I am deeply grateful. The annual meeting of the Catholic Biblical Association also occasioned opportunity to present two of these chapters in their early stages. These professional gatherings of colleagues always provided the impetus to strengthen arguments and deepen analysis of the project.

Administrative support and interest from my associate dean and colleague, Alison Benders, has been a steadying presence along the way. Particular graduate students, Sarah Kohles, Lisa Hui, Seumaninoa Puaina, and

Yoon Kyung Kim, all read and commented on various chapters. Tae Wong Lee offered assistance when difficulties arose with technology. And my daughter, Hannah Hens-Piazza, who is forever my fearless critic, read and made invaluable comments on several of the early drafts. Late in the game, Steven McKenzie read and offered important feedback on the final draft. I am deeply grateful for his early encouragement to expand and publish this work and, later, for his willingness to review the manuscript in such detail. Finally, this project would not have come to completion without the skill and editorial imprint of Nancy Haught. For her unremitting attention to detail, care for every word on each page, and especially for her friendship, I am forever grateful. As always, I am in debt to my family—Fred, Hannah, and Gabriel, who put up with my all-too-frequent status of "missing in action" but are always there to support my work.

Chapter One

Making a Case for the Supporting Cast

The Bible qualifies as a powerful force in contemporary culture.[1] Directly and indirectly, it inspires, entertains, informs, contradicts, and remains present in both expected and unexpected ways. Certainly, across both Jewish and Christian communities, the Bible participates as a formative player, as a partner in discerning doctrine and ethics alike. But also in various other sectors of our culture and before people who have never opened its covers, the Bible manifests its cultural importance in a host of influential representations and commodifications, ranging from the sublime to the absurd. From Caravaggio's *Sacrifice of Isaac*, to Michelangelo's Sistine Chapel, the Bible as a subject of art has been unsurpassed. Works like Handel's *Messiah* suggest the Bible's influence upon musical scores and productions. Whether as intertextual partner in Dostoyevsky's works, as subject for imagery in Gerard Manley Hopkins' poetry or as analogue for popular fiction like Anita Diamant's *The Red Tent*, biblical stories and themes echo frequently across cultural and literary works. Then there are those absurd commodifications of the text—chocolate tablets of the Ten Commandments, board games such as Bible Trivia, and Jello molds in the shape of Noah's Ark, with all the animals it contained. Hollywood, too, has had its share of the prize when it comes to the Bible. Disney's *The Prince of Egypt*, Cecil B. DeMille's *David and Bathsheba* and Mel Gibson's *The Passion of the Christ*, as examples, indicate the vast scope of these cinematic overtures. Without a doubt, the Bible remains embedded in a whole variety of cultural manifestations, suggesting the here-to-stay status of this ole book.

On a more serious note, all of us are keenly aware of the Bible's authoritative intonement down through the ages. It has been mined to authorize theologians' understandings of the sacred. It continues to be quoted to justify politicians' positions on moral matters. It has been enlisted to support nations in their imperialistic land grabbing escapades. At the same time, it has been called upon to underwrite liberation campaigns aimed at overturning such colonizing regimes. Even today, the controversy over territory that has kept some people hostage and others at war or living in fear stems from a biblical tradition about land and to whom it was bequeathed. Whether marshalled as ally or enemy, the Bible is accorded an authority that, even in this twenty-first century, makes it a powerful cultural force. All this should serve as a warning: Failing to recognize, or at least grant the Bible its influence in culture today, will not curtail the Bible's influence.[2]

SUPPORTING CAST VS. SUPPORTING CASTE

In conjunction with this cultural significance, the impact and intrigue of characters from the Judeo-Christian Scriptures are well known. Though far less complex than the characters we encounter in contemporary literature, biblical players influence culture as they motivate, entertain, or even inspire readers in their own lives. So enormous is the impact of many biblical heroes and heroines that they frequently burst off the page and, as already noted, become the subjects of colossal sculptures, steamy novels, massive paintings, magical operas, and Hollywood blockbusters.

The ongoing fascination with biblical characters underwrites this study and proposes a two-fold agenda defining its scope. First, it sets forth in-depth analyses of several biblical characters from this complex of ancient stories. However, it turns away from the major characters that typically command our attention. Instead, it shifts attention toward those players in the biblical tradition who are frequently referred to as "minor characters," that is, that vast cadre of individuals in the narrative who, from now on, will be referred to as the "supporting cast." These are the players in biblical narratives whom interpretations often pass over. Frequently considered as part of the background, these characters are typically viewed as props. Often, they are thought to exist solely for enhancing the characterization of the protagonist. Though present in the narrative, the story of the supporting cast is never told. Instead, they appear only to shoulder the burden of a story that is never their own. Indeed, at first glance, a brief assessment suggests just how slimly drawn these characters actually are. Without a more prolonged look, one could legitimately question if they can actually be studied at all.

However, this study wagers the value of such a prolonged look. Believing that every story tells many stories, it searches the narrative for clues that hint at the contours of a supporting cast member's story embedded in the text. Such an approach considers not only what is included but what has been left out. It looks for counterparts in other stories that might thicken a thinly sketched portrait. Such an investigation not only considers what might be the literary abundance gleaned from such scrutiny; it also attends to another kind of yield stemming from such an effort.

More specifically, as a second objective, this project also attends to the social and cultural capital resulting from reading practices focused upon the supporting cast. Aided by scholarship from the sociology of reading,[3] this endeavor rests upon the assumption that a dynamic relationship exists between our reading and interpretation habits when it comes to texts and our practices of engagement and interpretation when it comes to our world. How we read important cultural texts influences how we read our world. At the same time, how we read and interpret our world influences how we read and understand important cultural texts, like the Bible.[4] Fixing attention only upon "major characters" in stories does more than cooperate with the hierarchy of the narrative or support the caste system of a story. It may reinforce and validate a similar perception of our own social world. By contrast, enlisting a more inclusive approach to reading, which attends not only to protagonists but also to members of the supporting cast, may shift attention, or even cultivate sensitivity, to their counterparts in our surroundings. Hence, the analysis of these supporting cast members invites readers to reflect upon whether the hierarchy embedded in the narrative world, which privileges some characters over others, and even the hierarchy of our literary designations (major vs. minor) may be related to classism, hierarchies, or "caste" categories that often order the perception of the world in which we live. Analysis of these supporting characters will disclose the new gains that might result from more democratized reading practices, as well as highlight what would be lost if this group continues to be overlooked. Hence, new insights about these often ignored characters will not only enhance our understanding of these biblical stories but also subtly summon readers to consider whether how we read the Bible really matters.

Three brief discussions offer an introduction to this study. First, a general consideration of the anatomy of the supporting cast in biblical narrative poetics will be set forth. Second, an overview of the poetics of supporting caste in the politics of the narrative will follow. Finally, this chapter concludes by taking up the politics surrounding reading practices: supporting cast versus supporting caste.

THE ANATOMY OF THE SUPPORTING CAST IN BIBLICAL NARRATIVE

When the supporting cast in biblical narrative is acknowledged in the literature, scholars either refer to them as "minor" characters or they are not referenced at all. Often falling outside the specifications of literary categories, these characters are less likely to be studied. The problem stems, in part, from the lack of consensus about nomenclature in characterization studies. Classifications of characters are themselves varied and problematic. During much of the twentieth century, most discussions on character were guided by E. M. Forster's categories. Characters are either major or minor, round or flat, protagonists or antagonists.[5] Clayton Hamilton's influential work does not disregard Forster's groupings but defines characters further as either static or kinetic, depending upon their relation to the action of the tale.[6] Baruch Hochman promulgates other lenses by which to view these individuals in the story world, casting them as opaque or transparent, literal or symbolic.[7] Seymour Chatman attempts to replace the polarities plaguing character categorization (major/minor, static/kinetic, literal/symbolic) with a continuum. He reframes character as a "paradigm of traits" communicated directly or indirectly by the narrator, other characters, the setting, or even an interpreter.[8] In turn, this collation of features yields a character whose rank is determined by his or her importance to the action of the story. While advancing the discussion beyond the oppositions of earlier taxonomies, Chatman's theories expose the presumed hierarchy in the narrative system. A character's worth or importance is determined by his or her relation to the action of the story, or the number of words recited by them or about them.

Reception theory that features the reader in criticism complicates the discussion further by questioning whether a character's importance is a product of production or reception of the text. Hence, the turn to the reader brings another set of considerations that further compound our take on character. The influence of Soren Kierkegaard's understanding of the self, as that which is discovered and disclosed in the presence of the other, suggests that the more said by and about a character, the more the reader has access to that individual.[9] Others, like Norman Holland and Wolfgang Iser, would argue the opposite: The less said about a character, the more readers must supply to fill in his or her contours.[10] Michel Bakhtin's conception of character in the novel seems, at first, to straddle both sides of the argument, contending that the development of the character occurs both within the text and beyond it.[11] For Bakhtin, character rests both on the assumption of reception and on the quantity of what the narrative (in his case, the novel) yields about a character. However, Bakhtin's privileging of composition in the development of character becomes clear. He argued that "the human being in the novel is, first and foremost, always a speaking human being. . . ."[12] Presumably, the more characters speak, the more they become marked by what Bakhtin calls "transgredience," a consciousness that results from that essential "dialogic" relation with other characters in the text.[13]

For many members of the supporting cast in biblical narrative, none of these categories adequately frames their construction or role within the story. In most literary classifications, they are referred to as minor characters, but they are not minor in the classic sense of literary categories. In the most minimalist sense, they are even less than what is traditionally thought of as minor characters. At best, they are like Forster's flat characters who, though they have a role to play, receive minimal descriptive attention by the narrator and so reside in a most constricted space of the narrative. The difficulty encountered in classifying these very minor characters in the Bible might stem, in fact, from the distinctiveness of biblical narrative itself.

Years ago, Robert Alter noted a real curiosity about biblical narratives that challenges the notion of characters being equal to the sum of the words in a given text or their importance to the action of the story.[14] He observed that while interpretations and representations outside the Bible tend to portray characters such as Moses, Esther, or David (main or major characters) with depth and complexity, they are in fact, by most literary standards, thinly drawn in their biblical story world. When compared to the sharply detailed portraits of personalities we encounter in Western literature or placed alongside the heroes of the great Greek classics, biblical characters (and, again, he was speaking about major characters) appear rudimentary. So, if even the most significant players of the Bible do not exactly qualify as major in contemporary literary terms, due to their narrative svelteness, it is not surprising that the so-called "minor characters" are even more elusive and harder to capture in the currency of contemporary literary categories. Accorded little or no description in the text, these minor characters do not conform to any of the familiar theoretical confines: they are not round or flat, protagonist or antagonist. Falling outside quantifiable frameworks governed by the number of words they recite or the words recited about them, there seems little to justify attention to them in interpretation. Entered into the story with the most economic description, their identity is rarely personalized. Often they are ensconced in a social category—"widow," "child," "foreigner," "servant"—or merely suggested by a collective reference—"villagers," "peasants," "enemy." Accorded only a few words, or often altogether voiceless, they serve as fixtures or agents, enhancing or advancing the action of a story that obscures them. Located somewhere in the junction between implied person and narrative form, they exist not so much on the margins of the story. Rather, the supporting cast lodge in the interface between story and discourse.

While they typically reside in the content of the tale, only an abbreviated appearance marks their time in the narrative. They may utter a few words to move the story forward. They may serve as collateral in a tense exchange between main players. Narrated discourse typically delimits and determines their existence. The form of the story may warrant they linger as accoutrements of the background or as animators of suspense. In some cases, once their function is fulfilled, they may quickly disappear. They may be "servants," who seek to address Saul's tormented spirit and procure David as a musician (1 Sam 16:14–17). They may be two starving mothers, depicted as cannibalizing their own children only to magnify the controversy between

Israel's king and the prophet Elisha (2 Kgs 6:23–31). Among their quiet ranks stands the unnamed midwife, who not only functions at the service of Tamar's complicated birthing of twins but also as an adjunct in the service of the larger story of Judah and Tamar (Gen 38:28–29). Some supporting cast members might exist only as a group to sketch in a populous setting or perform some task. The "skilled ones" commissioned by Moses to craft the tabernacle in the wilderness number among these collectives (Exod 35: 10f). The non-Israelite people conscripted for slave labor by Solomon qualify as one of these anonymous assemblages (1 Kgs 9:20–21). So might the "four lepers" who discovered the deserted camp of the Arameans (2 Kgs 7:3–11), saved the starving population in Samaria and thus highlighted the fulfillment of the prophet Elisha's word. Hence, the social dimensions of these very minor characters emerge not only in their reflection in the story's content but also by way of the inflection of their characters in the story's form. Their story is not told, their plight is never addressed, nor is the interest they might generate rarely fostered in interpretation.

Most critics view such characters as so minor as not to warrant attention or investigation. Percy Lubbock argues that they show such insubstantiality that there is little to study.[15] Wayne Booth ignores them altogether and deals with character in his work on fiction as primarily a succession of major figures.[16] William Harvey will study minor characters if they fit into his taxonomy of characters: protagonists, intermediate figures, and significant background characters.[17] However, years ago, Eric Auerbach, in comparing Homeric and biblical characters, recognized that what is background, left obscured, and unexpressed is loaded with multiplicity of meaning and presents fertile ground for interpretation.[18] More recently, Chatman also called character an occasion that provides for "an amplitude of associations," allowing space for consideration of even these very minor players.[19] What might be the yield if we train our attention on the supporting cast, allowing for their "multiplicity of meanings" or the "amplitude of associations" that they might conjure? What are the consequences if we ignore them?

THE POETICS OF THE NARRATIVE CASTE SYSTEM

Who are these biblical characters, members of a supporting cast? Fleetingly referenced, they are "the maidens dancing in Shiloh," who are kidnapped and taken for the Benjaminites as wives (Judg 21:15–24). They are the remaining "inhabitants of Gath, Gaza and Ashod" after Joshua's bloody campaign against the Anakim (Josh 11:21–23). Among their quiet ranks stand "the prostitute of Gaza," visited by Samson in his exploits against the Philistines (Judg 16:1–3); "a man of Baal-Shalisshah," who provided a loaf of bread for Elisha's miracle (2 Kgs 4:42–44); "the captain," who fell before Elijah to save his army of fifty (2 Kgs 1:13–16); or the "woman nurse" guardian, who protects Jehoash as a child (2 Kgs 11:1–3). Embedded in the text, these characters constitute the scaffolding of the story world. Though they provide the infrastructure upon which to build the narrative, their involvement often means effacement. Full development of the protagonist appears contingent upon the utilization and delimitation of these supporting cast figures. One of the most effective ways to ensure their delimited status and support the caste system of the narrative is to refuse them a name. In *Theory of Literature*, Rene Wellek and Austin Warren contend that naming is the simplest form of characterization. "Each appellation is a kind of vivifying, animizing individuating"[20] of a character. William Gass reinforces this observation with his definition: A character is, first and foremost, "the noise of their name and all the sounds and rhythms that proceed from them."[21] Even Roland Barthes speaks about name as the start of character.[22] Thus, denying a name to a character reflects the politics of the narrative. It qualifies as one of the foremost strategies for crafting the hierarchy of the story. Depriving characters the personal identification of a name discourages recognition of their significance or even presence in the story world. In fact, a brief overview of biblical narrative discloses that the majority of supporting cast members are not named. They are hardly visible, and rarely even heard. If they speak, they are silenced after the sentence or two they have been assigned. Often they are expelled from the storyline as soon as their function has been completed. Nameless, silenced, expelled, they are the subaltern of the literary world. Hence, their actual role unfolds a lot like those of the functionaries in a familiar political system: Marx's framework of utilitarianism. They provide a service, but the work they do covers over their exploitation in this labor system, in this case the narrative caste system. They are characterized only in light of their function—"servant," "guardian," "prostitute," "survivor," and "soldier." References to their person expeditiously convert them into abstractions of utility. Their identity as narrative functionaries serves to effectively efface any manifestation of human qualities. With sleight of hand, such narrative utilitarianism accomplishes a conceptual theft. The actual expropriation of center stage and character importance of the many is overshadowed and sacrificed for the sake of the few. Hence, these less-than-minor characters become the proletariat of the narrative world. They are the serfs of the narrative system, the subaltern of the plot, at the service of a storyline that is never their own.[23]

In popular literature, they might be the street vendor who sells flowers to the hero protagonist. Or in a contemporary novel, they could be sketched as an unnamed housekeeper, who for purposes of suspense, unknowingly pauses to check her watch outside the hotel room where a murder is underway. In the biblical tradition, such obscured personalities are also present, though often existing in the shadows or as mere suggestions in the storyline.

They are the occupants of the less desirable towns of Galilee that Solomon hands over to Hiram in exchange for gold and bronze to finish his extravagant temple and palace projects (1 Kgs 9:10–11). They are workers who weave clothing for Asherah, whom Josiah fires in an account of his efforts to centralize cult, allegiance, and tribute in Jerusalem (2 Kgs 23:7). They are the friends of Jephthah's daughter, fleetingly referenced in the text, who accompany her to the hills to mourn her unfulfilled life (Judg 11:39). They are the unnamed children about to be sold into debt slavery, whose widowed mother insists that the prophet protagonist Elisha assist her (2 Kgs 4:1–7). They are the peasants mentioned by Amos, whose subsistence farming is taxed beyond what it can endure during the reign of Jeroboam II (Amos 5:11a). They are the literary gears that drive the narrative forward. They perform functions at the service of those named protagonists about whom the narrator fixes attention and narrates the tale.

Given their status as mere functionaries, one could ask whether it is even legitimate to promote the supporting cast or assign them an importance beyond the literary task they perform in the narrative? Such expositions could appear as a violation of the text's hierarchy of values. Indeed, the characteristic label "minor" is already a value assessment, suggesting their delimited role while, at the same time, distracting the reader from the important part they might play. But still some might object: Isn't training our attention upon these lesser characters a disruption of the author's initial vision?

Attention to minor characters need not be an affront to how the biblical texts have been composed. Nor does such an inquiry suggest that authors might have composed their works differently. Instead, investigating the supporting cast recognizes the essential openness of a literary text. It invites readers to entertain the possibility that any narrative tells more than one story at the same time. Our reading practices determine what stories we tune in to. Thus, the decision and the responsibility for listening for the other accounts, (i.e., the stories of servants, survivors, war hostages, residents of towns bartered for gold and timber, etc.) reside with readers. Do we read past these characters and support the caste system of the narrative, or do we entertain the other stories that the supporting cast might have to tell?

POLITICS SURROUNDING READING PRACTICES—SUPPORTING CAST OR SUPPORTING CASTE?

The plot of any story features the characters resident there. How the narrative unfolds and its inherent poetics call attention to this process of emphasis and strategy, which spotlights some characters rather than others. Hence, the narratives themselves offer clues that suggest how a shift in emphasis might yield other possible stories and how other, fuller lives might find their way into the foreground. Alternate accounts are interwoven in the storyline. Though not featured by the narrator, the supporting cast are not just characters adjunct to the story. Without them, the plot would relate a different story or would tell less of a story. Often, members of the supporting cast are so significant that, in their absence, there would be no story at all. Without the unnamed "servant girl," who informs Naaman's wife how he could be cured, the military general of Aram would not have traveled to Samaria for a healing by the prophet Elisha (2 Kgs 5:2–3). And in that same story, without the wise cajoling of his unnamed servants, Naaman's arrogance would have prevented him from going down into the Jordan River, where he was finally cured (2 Kgs 5:13–14).

Recognizing the vital role of the supporting cast emancipates the reader from the caste system of the narrative. It engenders alternative reading practices, the kind that result in a more equitable assessment of all the characters in a story. This method requires that we take seriously the license and responsibility that reception theory has accorded us as readers. Despite their brevity in the text, whether actual or merely suggested, these characters manifest a remarkable quality. They persist in the reader's memory. Their brevity or insufficiencies as characters have a paradoxical effect upon the reader. Adopting here Iser's notion that "less is more," the less presented on the page, the more engaged the reader becomes. Hence, the realm of these very insignificant individuals offers an invitation for readers' deep involvement in a story. Indeed, readers themselves contribute dimension to characters by both identifying with them and supplementing their sketchy portraits with projections. Norman Holland notes, identification with a literary character is "a complicated mixture of projection and introjection, of taking in from the character certain drives and defenses that are really objectively 'out there' and of putting into them feelings that are really our own."[24] However, our participation in the construction of the characters is not a one-directional dynamic. Characters and their stories also play a role in the crafting of our world and our lives in it.

Years ago, Michel de Certeau in his essay, "Reading as Poaching," observed that what and how we write and read construct "the real" in our lives.[25] As in texts, so also in life. Both share the same power and the same limitation, namely, language. Once again, this means that how we read the Bible stands in close relation to how we read the cultural texts of our own world. The namelessness that enshrines some characters, the opportunity for speech that is denied to others, the delegation of some women and men as expendable, and the lack of social standing accorded to such characters as virgin daughters in these tales are all subtle, but nevertheless real examples of degradation and even violence. If we fail to cultivate a sensitivity toward these individuals in the story, we risk failing to cultivate a sensitivity to such persons in our own lives. Moreover, we also gamble our ability to recognize some of the unsung heroes of our own society, to take note of the uncelebrated examples of self-giving individuals in our surroundings, or to miss the subtle but nevertheless real occasions of abuse or valor that often unfold right before our eyes. This relationship between reading texts (in this instance, biblical texts) and reading and interpreting texts of our own culture is at the heart of this study. The choice to read the supporting cast or to support the caste system of the narrative summons readers to embark upon a self-examination about the consequences of our reading practices. Does the way we read sequester some characters in our interpretation who might challenge our partisan way of proceeding? Does how we read corroborate a narrator's version of an individual whose prejudices and short sightedness we share? Do our reading practices reinforce a fictitious sense of self in relation to what, in our own hierarchical system, are deemed the minor characters of our world?

Our sense of self is mediated by others. Those "others" are made up, not only of persons in life and on the page, with whom we are quick to identify or who seem most like us. Some of the most compelling insights about ourselves and what is possible for our lives will be prompted by those least like ourselves. Perhaps they reside among that supporting cast, which we might have been trained to turn away from or have been encouraged to ignore. Whether in life or in literature, reading only the central figures, those spotlighted by the narrator or those crafted as the tragic or comic protagonists, breeds a fallacious understanding of ourselves. Self-understanding demands an enormous range of characters to learn from and identify with. It seems that only then can we begin to achieve an honest assessment of our strengths and vulnerabilities, our virtues and vices, and our potentials and limitations.

How we grapple with the members of the supporting cast, whether in the biblical text or as they ricochet across the cultural texts of our world, saddles the reader with further responsibility. At first glance, epistemology appears inevitably yoked to ontology. What the texts say about character "A" is the very means by which character "A" exists. Since less information is provided about these lesser characters, their ontological pull upon us seems minimal. But if we take them seriously, do research to better understand their social standing, interrogate the text as to their minimization, and, based upon appropriate studies, consider their potential contribution, we begin to shoulder, as it were, the epistemological burden with the writer. Such an investigation and the resulting exposition thicken a slim character and, in turn, effect ontology.[26] As we shall see, one-dimensional readings zoom out and offer a three-dimensional view. New details, greater complexity, and other potential plots come into focus. In the process, new lives, previously deemed as "the other," assume center stage, commanding attention and understanding. In texts and in life, the existence of these sidelined individuals is brought into focus and into the foreground. In this new bold relief, they beckon recognition for our initiative.

Therefore, this study proposes an alternative way of moving forward when it comes to the biblical texts. It promotes a reading practice that grows out of literary theory in which categories of major and minor characters are abandoned. It seeks a solid artistic motive for all characters and their exposition in analysis. It aims for a more democratized assessment of the text, in which all characters deserve a hearing. The motive animating such interest eclipses mere literary intrigue. It presumes the relationship between the critical eye, trained to survey important cultural texts such as the Bible, and that same critical eye's attention to the presence and importance of (as it turns out) these not so minor characters in our own world. Thus, we can train our attention upon the supporting cast in the biblical stories, or we can support the caste system of the narrative and read past them. How we read the biblical text matters. Grappling with the broadest range of characters grants us urgently needed insights into the many and different "others" who make up our world. It redefines who among us are assigned to categories of privilege and importance in our private and communal schemes of reality. It gives us pause before those whose importance we might otherwise have missed. At this challenging juncture in the life of our fractured world's ever-shrinking global village, the value of such knowledge and understanding needs little explanation.

NOTES

1. As early as the 1990s, biblical scholars had begun to study the interaction between the Bible and culture as a discipline of the field. See for example J. Cheryl Exum and Stephen Moore, eds. *Biblical Studies/Cultural Studies* (Sheffield, UK: Sheffield Academic Press Ltd., 1998), a work that grew out of the third colloquia on the intersection between the Bible and culture.

2. When considering the Bible's role in culture, Regina Schwartz, *The Curse of Cain: The Violent Legacy of Monotheism* (Chicago: University of Chicago Press, 1997), 8, goes so far as to warn that "if we do not think about the Bible, it will think (for) us."

3. Among those contributing to the current field of study are Peter Smagorinsky, "If Meaning Is Constructed, What Is It Made From? Toward a Cultural Theory of Reading," *Review of Educational Research* 71, no. 1 (2001): 133–69; R. J. Tierney and P. D. Pearson, "Towards a Composing Model of Reading," *Language Arts* 60 (1983): 568–80; and J. Wertsch, *Voices of the Mind: A Sociocultural Approach to Mediated Action* (Cambridge, MA: Harvard University Press, 1993).

4. In "Negotiating What Counts: Roles and Relationships, Texts and Contexts, Content and Meaning" in *Linguistics and Education* 5 (1993): 241–74, Ana Floriani discusses how reading itself is a constructive act, carried out in conjunction with all kinds of texts. Specifically, Floriani notes the interactive relationships between how one reads a text and how one reads that same reader's context, which she calls "intercontext." Similarly, Smagorinsky notes that reading is a constructive act, lived through a process of association into a response in a reader's context, 149.

5. E. M. Forster, *Aspects of the Novel* (New York: Harcourt & Brace, 1927), 60–78.

6. Clayton Meeker Hamilton, *A Manual of the Art of Fiction* (Garden City, NY: Doubleday, 1918), 116.

7. Baruch Hochman, *Character in Literature* (Ithaca, NY: Cornell University Press, 1985), 89.

8. Seymour Chatman, *Story and Discourse: Narrative Structure in Fiction and Film* (Ithaca: Cornell University Press, 1978), 118–20.

9. Soren Kierkegaard, *Soren Kierkegaard's Journals and Paper*, Vol. 4, trans. Howard V. Hong and Edna H. Hong (Bloomington: Indiana University Press, 1975), 4.634.

10. Norman N. Holland, *the Dynamics of Literary Response* (New York: W. W. Norton, 1975), 278, and Wolfgang Iser, *The Act of Reading: A Theory of Aesthetic Response* (Baltimore, MD: Johns Hopkins University Press, 1978), 119.

11. Michel Bakhtin, *The Dialogic Imagination: Four Essays*, ed. Michael Holquist, trans. Caryl Emerson and Michael Holquist (Austin: University of Texas Press, 1982), 32.

12. Ibid., 332.

13. Michel de Certeau, *The Dialogic Imagination: Four Essays*, ed. Michael Holquist, trans. Caryl Emerson and Michael Holquist (Austin: University of Texas, 1983), 32.

14. Robert Alter, *The Art of Biblical Narrative* (New York: Basic Books, 1981), 56.

15. Percy Lubbock, *The Craft of Fiction* (New York: The Viking Press, 1957), 68.

16. Wayne C. Booth, *The Rhetoric of Fiction* (Chicago: University of Chicago Press, 1983).

17. William J. Harvey, *Character and the Novel* (Ithaca, NY: Cornell University Press, 1966), 54.

18. Erich Auerbach, *Memesis: The Representation of Reality in Western Literature* (Princeton, NJ: Princeton University Press, 1953), 23.

19. Chatman, 115.

20. Rene Wellek and Austin Warren, *Theory of Literature* (London: Cape Publishers, 1966), 226.

21. William Gass, *Fiction and the Figures of Life* (Jaffrey, NH: David R. Godine, 1978), 49.

22. Roland Barthes, *S/Z: An Essay* (New York: Hill and Wang, 1974), 92.

23. See Alex Woloch's discussion on a Marxist labor theory of character in *The One vs. the Many: Minor Characters and the Space of the Protagonist in the Novel* (Princeton, NJ: Princeton University Press, 2003), 26–30.

24. Holland, 278.

25. Michel de Certeau, "Reading as Poaching," in *The Practice of Everyday Life,* trans. Steven Randall (Berkeley: University of California Press, 1988), 165–76.

26. See the more extended discussion of how this ontological pull becomes an epistemological burden for the reader in David Galef, *The Supporting Cast—a Study of Flat and Minor Characters* (University Park: Pennsylvania State University Press, 1993), 12–13.

Chapter Two

Foregrounding the Backstory

For centuries, the construct of character was not a central consideration in the analysis of narrative. Likely due to the influence of Aristotle, who emphasized the primacy of action, character was assigned a secondary significance.[1] With the early dawn of narrative studies in the eighteenth century, character was still but a dimension of plot, alongside theme, narrator, and stylistics. Attention to the construction of the novel during the nineteenth century, however, tipped the scales. Character began to move to center stage. With the work of critics like Henry James, character started to receive its rightful due. In his now classic "The Art of Fiction," James noted that "What is character but the determination of incident (action or plot) and what is incident (action or plot) but the illustration of character."[2] Echoing a shift taking place among literary critics of his time, James' work heralded a significant change in the working assumptions of literary studies. Character was no longer a dependent element of plot or the product of an impartial narrator. Character began to be considered a central and complex construction for scrutiny in narrative analysis. Soon becoming the dominant focus of research during the twentieth century, character now enjoyed an endless host of methodological approaches. It could be subject to psychological scrutiny. It might be assessed as a semiotic sign. Or character could be investigated as an intertextual prompt. Today, though a variety of diverse approaches continue to enshrine the study of character, mainstream literary critics all tend to agree not only on its centrality as locus for study but also on a working definition for character.

Character in literature exists as a two-fold development. First, it emerges as the product of the text. That is, it arises literally from a word or the words that, as a first draft, textualize a character's presence in the narrative. This textualization includes the descriptions of a character, what a character says or thinks, and what others in the story say about the character. Exchanges between characters, what the narrator relates, and what a story discloses—even indirectly—about a character's presence all contribute to this first take on the character's portrait. Second, but simultaneously, a character also exists as the effect of the reader and the reading process.[3] A character develops as a direct result of the impact of textual indicators inferred by the reader. Therefore, character might be defined as any textual trace suggestive of a person(s) that can impact a reader. This broadens the horizon of what qualifies as a candidate for study. Not only the so-called major characters, but also the multitude of other characters fashioned from a mere textual trace that effects a reader, are now legitimate grounds for scrutiny. Such an understanding serves as the basis for an in-depth study of the supporting cast. Once thought to be background figures, mere functionaries, etched in the margins or only implied in the story line, members of the supporting cast emerge and invite serious analysis. And, like other characters who have claimed the analytical spotlight for centuries, members of the supporting cast may also occasion inspiration, revulsion, challenge, or affirmation in those who take the time to study them.

As a product of the text, this motley cadre of individuals may appear as well-defined individuals with an abbreviated appearance or be present in the narrative to make only a brief statement. They may also exist merely as a set of traits, qualities, and descriptions. Recitation or services rendered craft these characters as individuals or as collective identities. They can evolve out of an adjective, an attribute, an action, or a predicate.[4] Indeed, the supporting cast's appearances and significance seem all but cursory at first glance. They appear to perform only one function in the story and then often are quietly dismissed. Because they have not merited the study they deserve, we may know them only by the defined task, career, role they fulfill in the story. In the narrative, they may appear to function as a foil. Sometimes they seem to exist only to display a value. Or they may be identified simply as the catalyst for an outcome in the plot. Frequently, the supporting cast is viewed as peopling the landscape, solely in the service of establishing the setting. For example, their mention as "the subjects" might be viewed simply as aiding the description of a king's court. Or a reference to them as "inhabitants" might be heard as subsidiary in a narrative focused upon a plundered territory or town. Or their notoriety as "the laborers" might be misunderstood as merely a passing detail in the more important story of a ruler's building enterprise. But their portrait emerges not only by what information or textual traces sketch or suggest their presence; the information that is missing or that which is withheld can also reveal much about characters. In addition, inferences from words, descriptions, and relationships to other characters may fill in their descriptions. Echoes from their counterparts in other texts can also thicken what we know about supporting characters. Moreover, how and when the narrator shifts attention toward them or away from them adds dimension to what we apprehend on their behalf. Taken together, the possibilities of inferring traits from textual indicators, in the intertextual echoes, the cues from the narrator, and even from the relationship between what is revealed and what is left out about these characters are infinite.

Like all characters, the construction of the supporting cast emerges not only as the product of textual traces. In the hands of the reader, any character and, as we will see, especially members of the supporting cast eclipse the textual confines. Inspired by his early predecessor, Roman Ingarden (1931),[5] Wolfgang Iser insisted in the 1970s on the role of the reader in constructing the literary work.[6] Reader response theory is concerned with how our sense of what exists in the text is generated not solely by what's in the text but also by our activity in appropriating or realizing it. The emphasis on a reader's activity is crucial, because it reminds us that the whole, which is the literary work, is not only the sum of its parts, or more than the sum of its parts; it is also a conjuring of absent or nonexistent parts. Along these lines, character is more than a sum of the words in the text about or spoken by the characters themselves. Moreover, every reader is distinct. Each individual comes to a text with his or her own idiosyncratic qualities, cultural sensibilities, and ways of seeing and processing what is read. Whether a character enjoys prolonged time and space in the narrative or only an abbreviated appearance, the reader plays a part in the characterization that results.

For example, when King David is strolling on his roof one evening he sees a woman bathing. First, he inquires who she is and then he commands his officers to go and bring her to him. Identified as Bathsheba, she is described only as "beautiful." The single word "beautiful" does not really give much information or create a very defined image of what David saw when he looked out from his roof at her (2 Sam 11:2). We don't really know what she looked like. We don't know why David considered her "beautiful." Was it because she was young and svelte or mature and voluptuous? The narrative records no description of her hair color or height. No information of whether maid servants assisted her during her bath or whether she saw David looking at her. Yet, prompted by this exceedingly brief textual description "beautiful," countless interpreters and artists seem to have to gotten a substantial impression of just what David saw. Based upon these few verses, Bathsheba has been the subject of numerous and elaborate artistic representations founded on David's voyeurism and that of subsequent generations of readers.[7]

Given their abbreviated description, how is it that biblical characters such as Bathsheba are endowed with such rich and complex character hoods in the tradition of interpretation whether in art, film, or literature. Why are they so recognizable, so vivid, so indelible? How is it that they are so well known? Contemporary literary theory argues that characters do not live completely or exclusively in a text. They are much more than what the text supplies about them. Their textual imprint is only an initial draft. The reader also plays a significant and integral role in fashioning the players in stories.[8] This is true not just of biblical characters, but of all the heroes and villains, protagonists and antagonists, so-called major characters and minor characters across the vast landscape of literature.

This recognition of the reader's role is so significant that it has caused a shift in character studies in the broader literary marketplace. Jeremy Rosen notes that "All of a sudden, they (minor characters) are taking over the popular literary landscape."[9] Moreover, this turn to minor characters is not limited merely to the more extensive analysis they enjoy in narrative interpretation. Contemporary writers are "seizing minor figures from the original texts in which they appeared and recasting them in leading roles."[10] Among numerous examples, Rosen cites the retelling of Shakespeare's *King Lear* from the perspective and social position of Lear's jester in Christopher Moore's *Fool*.[11] In another work, the Pulitzer Prize-winning *March*, author Geraldine Brooks features the absent father from Louisa May Alcott's *Little Women*, making him the protagonist.[12]

In this study, the analysis of the supporting cast will not eclipse the biblical text and what it reports. They will not become the subject for novels. Working with the assumption that every story tells many stories, the development of the supporting cast will remain faithful to what the biblical text yields, while recognizing that the reader has an opportunity to play a pronounced role in their characterization. While the text provides an initial trace or reference to "the slave," "the mother," "the two children," the reader and her research subsequently supplies draft upon draft each time she encounters these individuals in their story realm. Such characters are, at first, the outcome of the words in the text, but their development does not stop there. It is also fashioned, elaborated, and even thickened during the reading research process. Nor is it limited to the quantity of words on a page. When characters sketched in a story encounter a reader, they eclipse the meager biblical depiction and undergo vast and elaborate redrawing. While getting to know them, readers try to "figure them out" and read between the lines. Readers can ask questions that the story does not pose. They can note details not featured by the narrator. The potential for a more in-depth understanding of a supporting cast member also depends upon readers' familiarity with counterparts in other biblical stories or knowledge of the sociopolitical information regarding the role of the particular character. Both allow readers firm ground on which to predict a character's unnarrated action or response or even propose the feeling they might have had. Gathering all this information allows readers to develop expectations of characters or construct notions of what they might be like interpersonally. Impressions based upon not only what can be known explicitly, but also upon what can be surmised or what is implied from the textual evidence, contribute to the deepening of a character. What is not supplied by the texts can often be based upon further research about a character's role, what he or she says, or the context in which he or she functions in the story world. Here, the analysis might enlist the yield from other critical methods. Social roles, cultural customs, or a presumed historical context as informed by social science or historical studies can also inform the character analysis. Even text critical studies may clarify a dimension of a story that further enables our access to a more in-depth grasp of what we can know about a supporting cast member. The results of such diachronic approaches not only supplement what we typically define as a literary or synchronic study of these supporting cast members. This additional information can confirm, supplement, refine, or even correct what a reader first thought, and thus the character undergoes further revision. Moreover, the questions a reader asks may often be instigated by the ideological orientation of that reader to the story or what they perceive is the story's own embedded ideology. Therefore, the study of these minor characters further accommodates a variety of methods. In excess of the traditional contours of literary analysis of characters, readings that are feminist, liberationist, queer, postcolonial, ecological, and so on, all become fair game.

Soon even a character like Bathsheba is more than just the text's vague description "beautiful" (2 Sam 11:2). Bathsheba is looked at during her bath in her own court. Reading what the text does not include, nothing indicates that she invited this viewing or knew about it. In fact, given the privacy surrounding a woman's act of bathing, there is much to suggest that David's act would have been considered an intrusion of her privacy, likely against her will. Bathsheba does not act in this brief story. She is never the subject of a sentence. She is sent for and slept with by this king. The first and only time we read that Bathsheba says anything occurs at the end of this episode. She sends word to the king: "I am with child" (11:5) as the result of their encounter. Given the culture of monarchy, the reader may begin to feel the weight of the subjugation experienced by citizens ruled by such a monarch. Hence, one easily imagines the fear that occasioned Bathsheba's inability to resist, to say no, or to say anything to a king's order. Reading between the lines, some readers might relate Bathsheba to other subjugated women they know or have read about. Thus, empathy might surround Bathsheba as a woman violated. But the reader's empathy does not stop there. In the next episode (2 Sam 11: 6–21), when David hears that Bathsheba bears within her the evidence of his misdeed, he schemes a cover-up. He sends for Uriah, her husband, who is away at a battle, dutifully fulfilling his military obligation. The king anticipates that Uriah will return home to his house and immediately want to sleep with his wife. However, David's ploy to pass off evidence of his paternity fails when Uriah refuses to stay in his own home while his countrymen are still fighting on the front lines. The sadness a reader might assign Bathsheba multiplies when it is learned to what lengths this king will go to cover his adulterous tracks. Desperate but determined, David orders that Uriah be put in the front line of battle and killed. Not only has this woman been violated and impregnated by this ruler, she has also lost her husband. Hence, the abbreviated and general description of Bathsheba in the text as "beautiful," supplemented by her report of pregnancy, is now extended and elaborated by a complex and conflicted interiority. With even a marginal awareness of violence and its victims in our contemporary world, a reader would recognize patterns between what is known from current experience and what is read in the text. Gradually, an emotional life of affliction and trauma might be infused into this otherwise thinly drawn character named Bathsheba, described in the text only as "beautiful."

Baruch Hochman refers to this process of character interpretation as "reading out" characters from their context.[13] Ironically this "reading out" occurs as we "read in" to the text. We shape a character out of our experience, out of what is familiar, out of what rings true, and out of an amplitude of associations we bring to the tale. This idea suggests that the very nature of character is open-ended, subject to numerous fashionings and refashionings. The character is, in part, the vision of our speculation, constructed each time we come to a story. However, a character is not anything we make him or her to be. This is not an arbitrary projection of ourselves into the story, nor is it an extension of some unbridled fantasies rendering characters fit for the cover of tabloids or some award-winning fiction. Our speculations and constructions cannot overrun the story. The text sets limits upon our construction. The words of a text serve as the clay out of which we sculpt the character. While the experience we bring to the text will have a great deal to do with what we discover there, the character we encounter must begin with and be grounded in the text.

LITERARY THEORY AND LITERARY POLITICS

More than thirty years ago, the influence of postmodernism challenged the assumptions of cultural studies and paved new avenues for text study in the literary field. Jean-Francois Lyotard's charge of the "incredulity of metanarratives" not only raised questions about any theory claiming truth or the capacity of an idea to explain everything; it also nourished a growing suspicion that such grand narratives actually were suppressing counterclaims and might even be exercises of power to maintain *privileged* status.[14] Arguing for the emancipation of humanity, Lyotard posited the importance of the little narratives from individual lives that would allow for pluralistic ideas to preside in place of a single grand narrative.[15] Moreover, the promotion of individuals' "little stories" might be seen as a kind of campaign of resistance to foundational and totalizing claims of grand narratives.[16]

In literary studies, and more specifically in biblical studies, postmodernism fanned the flames of feminist interpretation, which were already well enkindled. Feminists had begun to disclose that the universalizing theological and ethical claims of the biblical literature were actually the assertions of patriarchal interpreters about a patriarchal text. In addition, postmodernism's emphasis upon the little stories served to validate the role of the reader, license reader response criticism, and recognize "much more complexity in the interaction of text and reader."[17] Hence, the credentialing of the "little narratives," coupled with recognition of the role of the reader, opened the gates and broadened the terrain of character analysis.

Two theorists in the field of literary studies have had particular influence in pioneering a shift in character analysis. In his book *The Supporting Cast: A Study of Flat and Minor Characters*, David Galef challenged the notion that major and minor were real or even legitimate divisions in which to cast characters in literature.[18] He argued that "minority is mostly a matter of viewpoint," not solely within the narrative but especially within the reader. Even though an author might only endow a character with a single trait and a momentary appearance in the narrative, the reader does not stop there.[19] For Galef, these minor characters in the "paucity of detail invite the reader's elaboration."[20] As much as Galef begins to emancipate these characters from their minority status, he does not go far enough. He continues to use the designation "minor characters" and even maintains that still "many minor and flat characters are simply meant as background."[21]

Alex Woloch, in his *The One and the Many: Minor Characters and the Space of the Protagonist in the Novel*, goes a step further and makes a case for the analysis of all characters in a novel.[22] He proposes a distributional matrix consisting of character space (the character's determined space and position within the narrative as a whole) and character system (the arrangement of different character spaces within the narrative), with which to study characters.[23] Such a template allows for the assessment of "how the discrete representation of any specific individual is intertwined with the narrative's continual apportioning of attention to different characters who jostle for limited space within the same fictive universe."[24] Of particular significance, is his labor theory of character. In speaking about minor characters, Woloch notes the "attempt to circumscribe a character within his or her delimited functionality is always potentially problematic.[25] Human beings represented in literary characters always constitute more than their function. If minor characters exist only to perform a function or facilitate development of a hero or protagonist in the narrative, this duplicates what in Marx's system constitutes utilitarianism's theft of experience. "Utility expresses the structural contingency of the bourgeoisie—in relationship to the exploitation of other human individuals."[26] Hence, defining some characters merely by their function effaces the "manifestation of definite qualities of individual having particular experiences."[27] Finally, Woloch wonders about the development of the existence of the "minor character" category itself. He writes, "If minor characters were *literally* minor in the normative sense of this word—'Comparatively small or unimportant: not to be reckoned among the greater or principal individuals of the kind' (*Oxford English Dictionary*)—the term itself would never have been formulated or deployed so often in literary criticism and evaluation."[28] Woloch acknowledges the narrative tension between what he calls the one and the many but also recognizes the importance of social inclusiveness as increasingly central to the novel and its interpretation.

This same social inclusiveness earmarks the politics undergirding this project and navigates our study of the supporting cast in biblical texts. A mimetic orientation toward texts maps the road ahead. Originally, mimesis innocuously viewed literature and works like the Bible as essentially an imitation of the various aspects of the universe.[29] It assumed a literary work reflected the world and evaluated it in terms of the truth or accuracy of this reflective interpretation. However, thirty years ago, a group of theorists, the New Historicists, challenged this static view and argued for a more dynamic understanding of mimesis that extends our understanding of what happens in "representation."[30] Imitation, when it manifests itself as representation, always involves a two-way process. It sets up a dynamic between two elements. As art imitates society, society imitates art. Hence, reading and interpreting literary works such as the Bible is understood as a mutual process of self-fashioning. Texts and their interpretation not only reflect life and make it possible for readers to understand what they read; life, society, mores, and culture itself are shaped by texts and what they inscribe. This is a process of mutual fashioning of society and literature simultaneously. In a similar manner, how texts are read and interpreted mirrors how society as text is read and interpreted. Who we attend to in texts, who we analyze, what we emphasize by our scrutiny, and what we ignore mirror and shape those same tendencies in our approach to our own society. In her monumental work *The Poetics of Postmodernism*, Linda Hutchinson summarizes it well. She writes, "How we read is not unrelated to how we see at least from the point of view of subjectivity."[31] In other words, how we read and interpret texts, especially important cultural or religious texts like the Bible, has a great deal of influence upon how we read and interpret the text of our world. Who we attend to, who we ask question about, or who we study in depth in texts seeds a similar interest in terms of who we see, who we inquire about, and who we seek to better understand in our own world. In addition, New Historicists have demonstrated that our interest in texts, even ancient texts, is always directly or indirectly tied to the present. The questions we ask about the past are inevitably tied to the questions we are asking ourselves about the present. Thus, it follows that the questions we ask about characters in stories are yoked to or grow out of questions we ask or need to ask ourselves about people in our lives.

As a consequence, this study of the supporting cast endeavors to invite a more democratized approach to reading. It aims to challenge the order of how we read and interpret texts and when necessary, disrupt the scale of our reading priorities and practices. Fixing the focus upon the supporting cast, it intends to redress the disproportionate amount of attention upon the so-called major players, the protagonists, or often identified heroes of the narrative. It intends to tell the little stories and to give voice to those characters from whom we have not yet heard. Attending to such previously disregarded literary subjects could give us access to a multiplicity of stories. It might urge readers to abandon social constructions of the story world that are one-dimensional and, instead, entertain those that are multidimensional and incommensurable. Readers would then be in better positions to abandon the social classism and establishment of a narrative, which prevent their hearing all the unheeded voices silently speaking there.

In the process, reading and interpreting biblical texts would disclose itself as more than an exercise in literary analysis when it comes to characterizing the supporting cast in the narrative. Acceding the multiple stories present there might reinforce or challenge the definitions and assumptions by which we understand people in our world. Becoming a practitioner of "stories from below" may counter or undercut the dominant story of the victor (main character) with that of the vanquished (the supporting cast). Attending to the supporting cast may disclose the way a society is. Or a consideration of the minimal placement or the silence of some in a story may prompt consideration of how a society ought not to be. With a focus upon the supporting cast, issues that are divisive in our world, that is, matters of class, capital, labor, race, gender, and so on, come into fuller view. What constitutes a hero, who really is virtuous, and where the subtle but nevertheless real violence rears its head all invite scrutiny with this narrative population. And, if shifting our attention to unnamed or previously unnoticed characters in important texts like the Bible actually can nudge us to create a more just and inclusive world, then we ignore the supporting cast at our own liability.

THE CASTE SYSTEM OF THE NARRATIVE

Studying the supporting cast of a story warrants addressing the factors that help to maintain the caste system of the narrative and discourage our attention to these participants. This hierarchical stratification of characters exists on two fronts—the caste system embedded in the story world and the caste system of our own analytical categories. First, in addressing the caste system of the story world itself, the namelessness that surrounds most of the supporting cast has already been mentioned. Though not all of these characters are without a name, a character introduced in the story without a name usually denies them worth or notoriety. But perhaps a more influential aspect of the maintenance of the narrative caste, beyond the anonymous identity of its supporting members, is the role of the narrator. Storytellers in narratives play a most influential role in determining who counts and who doesn't. In the narrative world, storytellers are actually the literary creation we call "narrators." They are the voices that tell the story, introduce characters, announce a change of scenes, navigate the plot, and offer concluding summations. Grammatically, narrators speak in the third person, telling the whole story as it unfolds. Their status as "emcees" gives us the impression that narrators are outsiders with objective perspectives.

For a long time, narrators and their status as storytellers have enjoyed an unearned confidence and credibility on the part of readers. Narrators have the authority to determine whose story is told, who has the privilege to speak, and who is rendered silent. Their third-person narration determines what is spoken and what is left unsaid. Moreover, narrators' third-person status gives the impression of an impartial authority in the story, a person whose perspective on the persons in the story and its events can be trusted. In the past, characterization theory exempted narrators from scrutiny. Narrators were protected from the suspicions, questions, and in-depth analysis we put to characters. We allowed narrators to decide what characters we knew most about and what characters we should ignore.

However, narrators are not authors. Like other players who make up the story, narrators are part of the textual world. Though more elusive, they themselves must be counted among the story's characters. Like other characters in the tale, they can be assessed based upon their words. Whom they attend to and ally with, how they relate an event, and what they choose to relate or withhold can craft an understanding of the narrator. Hence, though narrators may indicate by their descriptions, emphases, and fixations whom they deem as the important (major) players in a story, readers are free to make other assessments.

For example, in Exodus 2:15b–22, the seven daughters of a priest of Midian are shepherding their father's flocks when some men come along and threaten them. Moses, who happens to be in the region, defends the women, waters their sheep, and ends up being taken in, fed, and provided a wife by the women's father, Reuel. The narrator tells the story in a way that focuses upon Moses. The story opens with the narrator spotlighting him: "Moses fled from Pharaoh. He settled in the land of Midian and sat down by a well" (2:15). The narrator opens the story in such a way to indicate that this story is about Moses. Closing the tale, the narrator enlists the same iterative emphasis. "Moses agreed to stay with the man and he gave Moses his daughter Zipporah in marriage. She bore him a son and he named him Gershom; for he said, 'I have been an alien residing in a foreign land'" (vv. 21–22). Throughout this brief tale, the narrator tells this story as Moses' story. However, a critical reader might choose to resist the narrator's fix on Moses at Midian and, instead, show interest in the priest's unnamed daughters or in the daughter that was given away or in Reuel or even in the shepherds who threatened the women. So, a foremost strategy for studying the supporting cast involves resisting the narrator. The reader refuses to look and listen only where the narrator directs her attention. Instead, the resistive reader chooses to pay attention to all those spaces in the narrative where characters reside, in particular those not featured by the storyteller.

A second way that a caste system embeds itself in the narrative has to do with the nomenclature of character analysis. As already noted, literary theory traditionally has employed categories that connote a character's status in the story as "important" or "less important." Forster's elaborations of his categories, "round" or "flat" have been the starting point for various ways scholars have delineated what have come to be known as "major" and "minor" characters. Round characters are more thickly defined. Descriptions of their appearance, as well as narrations of what they do and what they say, work to craft their complexity and centrality in the narrative. Flat characters receive little elaboration and are one-dimensional, fashioned solely to represent a type or trait in the tale, existing marginally in the story. Citing M. H. Abrams's observation that still other characters who receive no description may exist solely in the narrative to serve a function, Adele Berlin proposed three categories of characters for the analysis of biblical texts and renamed them.[32] She calls Forster's round characters *full-fledged characters,* who "are realistically portrayed; their emotions and motivation are either made explicit or left to be discerned . . . from hints provided in the narrative." Berlin calls the flat character a *type,* who lacks much elaboration and comes off less as a real person and more of a blueprint of a trait or type such as a "wife," "mother," "king," and so on. Finally, Berlin proposes a third category she names *agent.* An agent achieves significance as character only in so far as they perform a function for the narrative or in the service of the plot. Berlin suggests we think about these categories as points on a continuum. But here's the problem. On one end of the spectrum exist the *full-fledged* characters who receive the greatest development and appear as she says, "like real persons."[33] Somewhere midway on the continuum exists the *type,* the character who takes on a typified role.[34] The definition of characters by recognition merely of the role they play or type they stand for means, at the same time, the bracketing of their person. It also sidelines their particularity, which would emerge if their unique story was recognized in the narrative. Finally, at the farthest extreme, exist the *agents,* "who are not important in their own right," but who have a function to perform in the service of the narrative construction or in the service of other characters in the plot.[35] Such a continuum not only encourages an interpretative hierarchy or caste system of analysis, it turns out that those characters who qualify as *agents* or *types*, the supporting cast, constitute the greatest number of characters in the biblical tradition. With their persons sidelined (*type*) or the view of them as mere functionaries (*agents*), the majority of characters are rendered merely the minority in the biblical texts. Sidelining them in literary analysis encourages this caste system in concert with their already diminished role in the story. Moreover, if, as our definition of character suggests, any textual trace affecting a reader signals a character, then, as we shall see, there are many members of the supporting cast who do not even enter into one of these categories and thus go completely unacknowledged.

THE SUPPORTING CAST: FOUR CATEGORIES[36]

No character is without complexity, purpose, or their importance, whether they appear briefly, assist in the unfolding of the plot, number among members of the "watching crowd," or participate as the implied occupants (men, women and children) of "the town destroyed by the enemy." While they all contribute to the story, their importance is determined not solely by the narrative, but also as the result of the reader who contributes to their fashioning. In other words, they exist, derive recognition, and are deemed worthy of attention only insofar as a reader grants it to them. It is also true of their counterparts in our world. They are visible, deemed worthy of recognition, and achieve importance only insofar as each of us cultivates a vision to see and acknowledge the significance of such persons in our own surroundings.

Who constitutes a real character or carries significance has little to do with how much of a role he or she plays in the narrative. Character is as much the product of readers as it is of the texts. Scholars of the tri-continental world, along with feminist interpreters, have long demonstrated that some of the members of the supporting cast are far more significant in the story than their minimal role or abbreviated appearance suggest.

Like the immense variety of individuals who inhabit our world, members of the supporting cast manifest a great variety in these stories. Borrowing a few terms from drama, four designations of character are offered here as an attempt to include a more comprehensive and inclusive roster of all the members of the supporting cast. The four categories include *complementary role*, *bit part*, *cameo appearance*, and *implied presence*.[37] While the groups reflect a somewhat quantitative relegation of characters' place in the narrative, the four designations do not signify any qualitative difference between the members of the groups. Regardless of the category to which a character belongs, each is worthy of study. Therefore, as a critique of the traditional politics of representation, their inclusion assumes that every character deserves a hearing.

Complementary Roles

Characters who might number as members of the complementary role group bulk largest in the narrative. Despite their less than front and center roles, they have staying power in the story. They often even receive a detailed introduction or have their own tale to tell. Many even have names. They wield a healthy hand in the story, often being responsible for a good amount of direct discourse. The narrator also makes mention of their presence and gives detail about these characters. Complementary characters directly influence plot, theme, and outcomes of the high drama unfolding there. They frequently prompt the dialogue and actions of other characters and even form a contrast to some of these players in the story. Typically, the narrative provides a good deal of information about them either directly, in the form of a detailed description, or indirectly, by virtue of their direct speech and action.

In a story about David, often titled, "Joab Negotiates the Return of Absalom," a wise woman of Tekoa (2 Sam 14:1–24) qualifies as a member of the supporting cast playing a *complementary role*. Though unnamed, she plays a key part in prompting David to assume his authority as king. She is a complex character who actually has two stories to tell. First, assuming the part of a widow, she tells a fictitious story for the purpose of nudging David to act on behalf of his exiled son Absalom. She controls the dialogue, initiating every exchange between the king and herself. Though the narrative seems not to be about her, she looms large and is essential to the unfolding of the plot. The unnamed woman's speech directly impacts King David and steers the story forward. The exchanges between David and this woman enable him to act on behalf of his son, as well as to begin functioning more assertively and appropriately in his role as king. Upon close scrutiny of her character, the woman's role is not minor or even secondary. She complements the narrative as well as demonstrates that the social distance and difference often assumed between such social categories as common woman and royal king are not what they appear. But this woman also has a second story to tell, her own story, when not pretending to be a widow. She is from Tekoa, a city not far from Jerusalem and known for its educational center. There is no indication that she actually is a widow but ample evidence that she has great audacity. That Joab enlisted her help indicates his dependence upon her to do what he cannot accomplish. Evidently, she was known for her persuasive powers, perhaps even before high authorities. That she succeeds influencing the king by her disguise and tale further suggests her skill as a compelling rhetorician. Though pretending to be his inferior, she boldly confronts the king, who we assume would be her superior. She skillfully employs idioms, patterns of speech, and tactics that were characteristic of folk wisdom, all of which suggest some kind of training or education. That she also speaks to the king about theological understandings registers as further evidence of her vast knowledge. In the story, she changes the course of events. And in her encounter with David, she changes the heart of a king. However, her goal seems not to be limited to the fate of Absalom. Her stated concerns eclipse her story and show her to be an "active trident of covenant values" (land and inheritance).[38] In the end, David's decision to bring back Absalom acknowledges her authority. Admittedly, this brief overview of her character merely scratches the surface of all that we might grasp from a more in-depth analysis of this complementary character. She deserves a full study. Yet even this little exposition suggests she has a bigger story to tell. Without a doubt, the authority, instruction, and insight of this woman, both in her disguise as a widow and in her real character as a wise woman, induces the king to rule wisely.[39] Labeling her by any designation that suggests her status as minor commits a great reductionism. In her significant role, the wise woman of Tekoa makes the story and its outcome possible.

Convinced that focusing upon her character sensitizes us to how and who we see in our own circumstances, we might ask who are her counterparts in our world? Who are the individuals that by their skill and wise speech cause others to flourish and make good decisions? How does she challenge the social hierarchies of the story? Does she help us consider whether the social hierarchies of our world are mere façades? What persons does she make us see in our own surroundings who make possible the accomplishments, successes, and maturation of others, but go unnoticed themselves?

Bit Parts

Other members of the supporting cast have *bit parts*, the second category of designation.

Characters with *bit parts* claim only a few sentences written about them or have minimal descriptions concerning their background, social standing, or role in the society implied in the story world. Their appearance is often brief and erroneously reduced in character studies to a mere function. But when those assumptions are sidelined, and their place in the narrative is given a prolonged analysis, their importance and significance often exceed their short narrative appearance. They frequently have a sentence or two in which to recite or ask a key question. Not assigned a large narrative space or prolonged appearance in the story, these bit-part players often appear and disappear quickly. Still, while their narrative involvement in the story is much more abbreviated than that of complementary characters, like the Tekoite woman, they have the same potential. They can change the course of the story, and they can even, in some instances, change the course of history. The major difference between them and other characters is a matter of the diminished narrative space they are afforded and the reduced air time that they are accorded. Though their time in the story is curtailed, they, too, play very significant and instructive roles despite their abbreviated appearance.

In 2 Kings 4:1–7, a brief tale relates the crisis of a widow who is in danger of losing her two children. She tells her story to the prophet Elisha. The two children are members of the supporting cast. They receive little description beyond the statement that they are about to be taken by a creditor as slaves to satisfy the debt of their dead father. No names, ages, or other information is provided about these two youngsters. They enter the story again, briefly, when the prophet instructs the widow to include her children in collecting jars to fill with oil. Again we hear of them when the widow, following the prophet's instruction, is pouring oil into jars in her house. Now their actual involvement is narrated: "They pass her the jars and she keeps on pouring" (2 Kgs 4:5). This time, the two children are referred to collectively with the third-person plural pronoun, "they." Finally, when the widow asks for another jar, it falls to one of the children to announce, "There are no more" (2 Kgs. 4:6). The proclamation and witness that the miracle is complete resonates from the speech of the child. While we don't know which child speaks, one of the two children with only a *bit part* assumes responsibility for announcing the achievement of the divine intervention. This child becomes the witness to the fulfillment of the promise to the widow, as well as to the salvation that lies ahead for all three of them. The children enter this brief tale a fourth time, as a reference in the prophet's speech to the widow after she conveys the results. He tells her to go and sell the oil and then pay off her deceased husband's debts. The prophet adds that both she and her children can live off the money that is left over. Though only members of the supporting cast, the children undergo a transformed existence. In the opening of the story, the threat surrounding them prompts the widowed mother to summon the prophet's help. "A creditor has come now to take my two children and make them his slaves" (2 Kgs 4:1). In the conclusion of the tale, the prophet assures the widow that she and the children will have a secure existence. "Go and sell the oil and redeem your pledge; you and your children can live on the remainder" (2 Kgs 4:7). Though members of the supporting cast, the children are at the heart of the crisis that reaches resolution. Their secured existence bears evidence of the scope of the miracle's effect. Though lacking the depth and narrative space of some of the other characters, the children are just as integral to the story, both for the construction of the plot and for the role they actually play. They are the reason necessitating the prophet's intervention. Both children assist in bringing his instructions to completion. One of them even bears verbal witness to the success of their work. Moreover, their restored well-being bears witness to the scope of divine intervention. To miss or ignore them, risks missing those less visible persons in our own world whose transformed lives bear witness of divine presence in our surroundings. Who are their counterparts in our age? Who are the individuals who discover abundance and well-being in life, despite very limited resources? Do we see them? And do we allow their tenacity amidst the most threatening of life's circumstances to challenge the fallacy that we are completely in charge of our own destiny?

Cameo Appearances

The third group of supporting cast members, those making *cameo appearances*, is the largest. They emerge from a mere name or job function, and they typically do not speak. Occasionally, they may offer a greeting or express some one-word response. Their identification in the story may be individual or collective. They might arise from an isolated look or a passing statement. They are "the laborers," "the quarrymen," "the spinners," "the soldiers," "the foreigners," "the slaves," and so on, who, when taken seriously, suggest the archaeology of the society embedded in the story world. It has long been assumed that these characters are simply meant as background. At best, they are thought to be literary props, scaffolding the scenery. Yet some of the most interesting examinations of these characters begin where other studies stop for apparent lack of an extrapolative base.

In the Book of Ruth, the "reapers" (*hakotzirim*), also referred to as "the young men" (*hanaarim*), are mentioned eight times (2:3, 5, 6, 7, 9, 14, 15) in the account of the first encounter between Ruth and Boaz in his field (Ruth 2:2-23). Other than a response to Boaz's greeting, they say nothing and receive no description. They appear in 2:3 and disappear in 2:17. These are the agricultural laborers on Boaz's land. Easily dismissed as literary props, their presence often is presumed to establish and detail Boaz's character, as one with property and wealth.[40] Further, the mention of his "reapers" or his "young men" in the field is routinely regarded as a means of amplifying Boaz's authority over a large constituency of employees.[41] Congruent with this status, Boaz's exchange with these field workers primarily takes the form of directives or a narrative about his orders to them. He tells Ruth he has commanded his young men not to molest her (v. 9). He also tells her she can drink from the water these young men have drawn (v. 9). Next, Boaz gives his reapers orders to "Let her glean among the sheaves themselves" (v. 15). He also commands them not to rebuke her for what she is doing or for what they have to do for her (v. 15). Further, he directs the young men to pull a few ears of corn from their bundles and let them fall to the ground so she can gather from them. Finally, he tells the field workers not to scold her (v. 16). Thus, the reapers are given clear mandates regarding Ruth. They are not to harm her (v. 9). They are to draw water for her to drink (v. 9). They must facilitate her work so she is successful (v. 15). And they must not shame her but treat her with respect (v. 16). Despite all the commands directed at them, we never hear from them. They are the silent collective referred to either as "reapers" or synonymously as "young men."

Though never narrated, "the reapers'" implied activity and response to Ruth is clear. She remains safe in what could be a hostile environment, even before Boaz comes on the scene. "So she went out and gleaned in the field after the reapers" (Ruth 2:3). Later, though never described or detailed, evidence of "the reapers'" obedient response to Boaz's orders, issued via his foreman, does materialize in the story. They evidently pulled out the sheaves from the bundles and left them for her to glean. Though the story never describes their response, at the end of the day, Ruth returns home to Naomi with "an ephah of barley," suggesting the virtue of these workers. Moreover, the implied but unnarrated action of the reapers on behalf of Ruth enables both Ruth and Naomi to flourish. And because Ruth is enlivened, rather than threatened, by them and their actions, her eventual offspring not only restores life to widowed Naomi; the genealogy at the end of the story indicates that it also paves the way to the Davidic line in Israel. Hence, this unnamed collective, "reapers," also vaguely referred to as "young men," have a hand in a very large project of divine design, that is, the continuance of Israel.

Who are their counterparts in our world? Who make up the hosts of individuals that contribute to the abundances of our lives but go unrecognized for the expenditure of their talents and labor? Failure to recognize their contributions cultivates a failure to recognize their person. Their behind-the-scenes work, contributions, and services may even be taken for granted. The virtue accompanying their steadfast labors gets missed. We risk becoming impoverished by such oversights, despite the abundance such workers afford us.

Implied Presence

The last group of the supporting cast in biblical narrative is made up of characters implied in the text, or what is being designated here as *implied presence*. One might ask what the smallest amount of information is that the text can provide out of which a reader can perceive a character? Since a character need not even be named to exist, any passing reference, or indirect statement or a phrase, or even an allusion establishes a point of reference. "Towns being destroyed" indicates slaughtered people. "Cheating in the marketplaces" implies cunning merchants. "Stones being quarried" suggests hard-working laborers. Stanley Fish would argue that the scope of the experiential base a reader brings to this reference determines the image of the character that develops.[42]

In this group of implied supporting cast members, the characters that emerge are the least able to lend themselves to a general analysis, as so much here rests upon the reader's sensitivity and experience. Even the identification of these *implied presences* is reader dependent. For example, a group of students may read the account of Josiah's religious reform (2 Kgs 23), where the king tore down all the local shrines, closed houses of prostitution, and shut down the houses where women were weaving clothes for Asherah. However, one reader among the group with an experiential base of living in the Alta Plano of Bolivia may wonder about all the peasants who lost their jobs as a result of Josiah's reform. The implied presences would be, therefore, the unemployed peasants who had previously run the local shrines, woven clothes for Asherah, or worked in the houses of prostitution. Who were the likely individuals who held these positions? In that society, what social position did they hold? How dependent was their livelihood upon these kinds of jobs? What was the consequence of the loss of this employment? How did the king's reform in the name of religion negatively affect the group of the already most impoverished class in that society? Do those in charge of large systems, government, or even religion today have responsibility to take note of the consequences, especially upon the least of a community, resulting from policy changes, new rules, or shifts in administrative decisions?

CONCLUSION

As theory shifts to accommodate consideration of the supporting cast, the scope for biblical interpretation widens. A given narrative no longer relates only one story but several stories, depending upon whom the reader decides to listen to and about whom the reader seeks to learn more. When the caste systems of both the narrative's construction and of the story world are abandoned, new lives come into focus. Examples of fidelity, friendship, loyalty, or other inspiring stories emerge in the texts. However, as we shall see, not all supporting cast members are virtuous. Just like their protagonist counterparts, some will manifest features of malice, selfishness, or even violence that are also too important to ignore. Whether motivating readers to fashion their lives in positive directions or serving as red flags warning readers what to stand against, these supporting cast members have an abundance to offer. They are, after all, the most populous group in literature and in the biblical tradition. Moreover, focusing upon them broadens our view, not only of the text but also of our own horizons. In the process, the yield of such a focus exceeds the texts. We become more sensitized and receptive to the counterparts of these supporting cast players in our own real-life surroundings. In the end, each reader will have to make the assessment whether such a consequence is worth the effort.

NOTES

1. Aristotle's *Poetics*, Trans. Kenneth A. Telford (Chicago: Regnery, 1961).
2. Henry James, "The Art of Fiction," in *Art of Fiction and Other Essays* by Henry James, ed., Morris Roberts (New York: Oxford University Press, 1948, originally published 1884), 3–23 at 13.
3. Tzvetan Todorov, "Reading as Construction," in *The Reader in the Text: Essays on Audience Interpretation,* ed. Susan R. Suleiman and Inge Crosman (Princeton, NJ: Princeton University Press, 1980), 67–82 at 77.
4. James Garvey, "Characterization in the Narrative," *Poetics* 7 (1978) 63–78 at 63; and Seymour Chatman, *Story and Discourse: Narrative Structure in Fiction and Film* (Ithaca, NY: Cornell University Press, 1980), 125.
5. Roman Ingarden, *The Literary Work of Art: An Investigation on the Borderlines of Ontology, Logic, and Theory of Literature,* trans George C. Grabowicz (Evanston, IL: Northwestern University Press, 1973), 250–254.
6. Wolfgang Iser, *The Act of Reading: A Theory of Aesthetic Response* (Baltimore, MD: Johns Hopkins University Press, 1978), 17–231.
7. See J. Cheryl Exum, *Plotted, Shot, and Painted: Cultural Representation of Biblical Women* (Sheffield, UK: Sheffield Academic Press, 1996), 19–53.
8. The work of Seymour Chatman, *Story and Discourse* (Ithaca, NY: Cornell University Press, 1978), and Baruch Hochman, *Character in Literature* (Ithaca, NY: Cornell University Press, 1985), have been particularly influential in reformulating a contemporary character theory stressing the role of the reader.
9. Jeremy Rosen, *Minor Characters Have Their Day: Genre and the Contemporary Literary Marketplace* (New York: Columbia University Press, 2016), 1.
10. Ibid.
11. Ibid.
12. Geraldine Brooks, *March* (London: Penguin Press, 2004).
13. Hochman, *Character in Literature*, 39.
14. Jean-Francois Lyotard, *The Postmodern Condition,* trans. Geoff Bennington and Brian Massumi. Theory and History of Literature 10 (Minneapolis: University of Minnesota Press, 1984), xxiv.
15. Jean-Francois Lyotard, "Lessons in Pragmatism," trans. David Macey, in *The Lyotard Reader*, ed. Andrew Benjamin (Oxford and Cambridge: Basil Blackwell, 1989), 132–33, 134.
16. Gina Hens-Piazza, "Lyotard," in *Handbook of Postmodern Biblical Interpretation,* ed. A. K. M. Adam (St. Louis: Chalice Press, 2000), 1647.
17. A. K. M. Adam, *What Is Postmodern Biblical Criticism?* (Minneapolis: Fortress Press, 1995), 18.
18. David Galef, *The Supporting Cast: A Study of Flat and Minor Characters* (University Park: Pennsylvania State University Press, 1993), 10.
19. Ibid., 14.
20. Ibid., 3.
21. Ibid., 11.
22. Alex Woloch, *The One vs. the Many: Minor Characters and the Space of the Protagonist in the Novel* (Princeton, NJ: Princeton University Press, 2003).
23. Ibid., 13–14.
24. Ibid., 13
25. Ibid., 26.
26. Ibid., 29.
27. Ibid.
28. Ibid., 37.

29. See the classic summary of mimetic theory from Aristotle onward in M. H. Abrams, *The Mirror and the Lamp: Romantic Theory and the Critical Tradition* (Oxford, UK: Oxford University Press, 1953), 8–14.

30. Stephen Greenblatt, *Renaissance Self-Fashioning: From More to Shakespeare* (Chicago: University of Chicago Press, 1980); *Shakespearean Negotiations: The Circulation of Social Energy in Renaissance England* (Berkeley: University of California Press, 1988); *Learning to Curse: Essays in Early Modern Culture* (New York: Routledge, 1990); and Catherine Gallagher and Stephen Greenblatt, *Practicing New Historicism* (Chicago: The University of Chicago Press, 2000). For the appropriation of New Historicism in biblical studies, see Gina Hens-Piazza, *The New Historicism*, Guides to Biblical Scholarship (Minneapolis: Fortress Press 2001); Stephen Moore, ed. *Biblical Studies and the New Historicism* (thematic issue), *Biblical Interpretation* 5, no. 4 (1997); and Daniel Boyarin, *Carnal Israel: Reading Sex in Talmudic Culture*, The New Historicism: Studies in Cultural Poetics, vol. 25 (Berkeley: University of California Press, 1993).

31. Linda Hutcheon, *The Poetics of Postmodernism: History, Theory, Fiction* (New York: Routledge, 1988), 168.

32. Adele Berlin, *Poetics and Interpretation of Biblical Narrative* (Winona Lake: Eisenbrauns, 1994), 31–32.

33. Ibid., 32.

34. Ibid.

35. Ibid., 85.

36. A version of the discussion that follows first appeared in an earlier form in Lúcás Chan, James F. Keenan, and Ronaldo Zacharias, *The Bible and Catholic Theological Ethics* (Maryknoll, NY: Orbis Books), 109–20.

37. While Galef, 12, continues to use the term "minor characters," he enlists three categories to talk about them: *cameos*, *bit parts* and *minor roles*. However, the categories of *cameo appearances* and *bit parts* that are proposed in this study digress from his use and definitions of these labels to represent members of the supporting cast.

38. See Claudia Camp, "The Female Sage in Ancient Israel and the Biblical Wisdom Literature," in *The Sage in Ancient Israel*, eds., J. Gammie and Leo Purdue. (Winona Lake, IN: Eisenbrauns, 1990), 189. On this point, Camp proceeds to caution against any arbitrary division between "so-called secular wisdom tradition and religious Yahwism."

39. For an extended study of her role in this story, see Gina Hens-Piazza, *Of Methods, Monarchs, and Meanings—A Socio-Rhetorical Approach to Exegesis.* (Macon, GA: Macon Press, 1996) 77–121.

40. Tod Linafelt, *The Book of Ruth.* Berit Olam: Studies in Hebrew Narrative & Poetry (Collegeville, MN: Liturgical Press, 1999), 30.

41. Tamar Cohn Eskenazi and Tikva Frymer-Kensky, *The Book of Ruth.* JPS Commentary Series (Philadelphia: The Jewish Publication Society, 2011), 31.

42. Stanley Fish, *Is There a Text in this Class? The Authority of Interpretive Communities* (Cambridge, MA: Harvard University Press, 1980), 34.

Chapter Three

Violence in Disguise

*A Study of a Complementary Character in
2 Kings 6:23–31*

Of all the members of the supporting cast, characters in complementary roles arise as the most visible and, at times, play pivotal roles in the narrative. Their steadfastness in stories coincides with a high level of influence that they are assigned in the unfolding of the plot. They wield a "healthy hand" in the major elements constituting a narrative. These characters often play an essential role in the build-up of narrative tension. Frequently, their part in the story aids in the disclosure of the main theme. Unlike many supporting cast characters, they tend to occupy a significant amount of narrative space. Complementary characters also speak and often have a sizable number of lines to recite when compared with the protagonist. They may recite lines or perform actions that instigate the central crisis in the plot inviting resolution. Hence, their characters and their development preside as essential to the storyline, making them integral to the narrative as a whole.

In addition, complementary characters conjure interest and intrigue. They linger in the reader's memory. An element of eccentricity tends to define their characters, making them memorable. Such irregularities may take the form of the comic, the grotesque, something peculiar, or just some unexpected trait that summons a reader's notice. Hence, these characters are worthy of study, not only because they often play key roles in the story, but because they also compel significant attention.

Like most members of the supporting cast, many of the members in this group are anonymous. Occasionally, they are given a name. Though they do not occupy the role of protagonist, complementary characters achieve a strange prominence in the narrative. Their interaction with the main characters is often intense and memorable. Frequently, they appear abruptly and grab more narrative space and attention than might be expected. On occasion, enough details are provided about them so that their own story constitutes a subplot. Perhaps because of their eccentricity, their speech or action may even claim the spotlight for an initial or short period in the narrative. Moreover, when they do speak or when their actions are described, what they say or what they do become integral to the unfolding of plot. And because they loom largest among the members of the supporting cast, the prospect for studying these complementary characters is immense.

AN ILLUSTRATION: 2 KINGS 6:24–33

The brief story unfolding in 2 Kings 6:24–33 resides within the larger literary unit of 2 Kings 6:8–7:20, which, in turn, belongs to the surrounding Elisha narrative.[1] Preceding our story, the prophet Elisha's directives to the king resolve one of the crises between Israel and Aram (6:21–23). At the conclusion of our tale, this same prophet's oracle before the king ends the famine (7:1–2). Thus, the words of the prophet serve as bookends, encircling and enclosing the story within. The content of the story also further confines this episode and its characters within the walls of a city. It begins by reporting, with unspecified historical references, that Ben-Hadad, an Aramean king, has besieged Samaria (6:24). Nothing can go in or come out of the city. Famine is wreaking havoc in Samaria. The story reports the consequences of this military assault, specifying both economic and domestic conditions. On the economic front, unsavory if not unpalatable foods, such as an ass's head and dove's dung, are commanding exorbitant prices.[2] Such economic conditions in the marketplace give way to an unthinkable desperation in the domestic sphere. A shift from third-person description to first-person speech magnifies and personalizes the gravity of the situation.

With the familiar salutation, "Help, O King," an unidentified woman beseeches Israel's king, who is walking on the wall (6:26) above her.[3] Without any inquiry, the monarch responds and incorrectly assumes that the woman seeks relief from the widespread conditions of starvation. He confesses his inability to help but absolves himself of responsibility for her suffering by defining the winepress and the threshing floor as God's domain (6:27). When he finally invites her to specify her request, the woman describes a different crisis, one that stems from the conditions of starvation but far exceeds them in gravity (6:28–29). An unthinkable controversy has erupted between herself and another mother after they agreed to eat their children. According to this woman's report, they have already boiled and consumed her own child, but now the other woman has broken the pact and hidden her offspring.

Though it is unclear what the woman is requesting of the king, his immediate response to the woman is twofold. First, he tears his robe. This public gesture exposes what he is wearing underneath his royal garments. "The people saw that the king was wearing sackcloth next to his body" (6:30). Second, and in the same moment, he pronounces a vow to kill Elisha, the prophet of God, whom he holds responsible for the conditions of starvation (6:31). Immediately, the focus of the tale shifts to the prophet's dwelling. Aware of the king's intentions and the messenger the king has sent, Elisha orders the doors of his house to be held shut (6:32). However, when the king himself arrives at the prophet's house, the monarch apparently comes to his senses and retreats from his threat.[4] Without explanation, we are told that the king has had a change of heart regarding the prophet. The monarch attributes the present conditions to Yahweh and confesses his despair (6:33).

Across interpretations, the controversy between the king and the prophet remains center stage, consistently taking precedence over and eclipsing the urgent crisis and desperate situation of the woman who has summoned the king. When this complementary character's crisis does receive attention, it is but a means to other ends. Her horrific story provides a motive for the king's hostility to Elisha. It illustrates the destructive behavior that prophets associate with rampant social breakdown.[5] It stands as grim "analogical contrast to a case brought before Solomon in happier days."[6] As the fulfillment of a Deuteronomic curse of disobedience (Deut 28:53–57), it conforms to the narrator's larger theological purpose: It narrates and illustrates the desperation of Samaria's citizens.[7] Finally, in its larger narrative surrounding, the story of this mother functions in some interpretations as merely a literary and theological prop in a plan that contrasts the waywardness of a king with the faith and integrity of God's prophet.[8]

But what might be disclosed if we fix our attention upon the complementary role played by this supporting cast member? What can be revealed if we study and interrogate her character? What are the contours of her story that are embedded in the narrative? And is there a lesson that might challenge us if we dwell upon her, instead of focusing solely upon the king and the prophet? The brief story told by this woman inscribes a thick subplot about herself and the life of some of the residents in a city under siege.

First, she is a mother who had a child. No information exists about whether she had other children. In ancient Israelite society, being a mother was the means by which women defined their worth and role in society. It also granted them status and provided security, even when a husband no longer existed or was present in the home. Children were the women's responsibility, and their presence in the home marked the domestic sphere as the domain over which women had some control. Here, children were socialized, taught the lore and customs of the community (Prov 1:8, 6:20). In the home, children were also steeped in the story of God's relationship with the people

(Exod 10:2, 12:26, 13:8; Deut 4:9, 6:7, 20–25, 32:7, 46). Even though most of the authority in the home rested with the father, the mother quietly, but most formatively, contributed to children's self-understanding as members of the community in the privacy of the home.

The narrative description of this woman offers no mention of her being identified with a husband. The agreement she makes with the other mother suggests this woman's sole decision-making capacity over the fate of her child, apart from any husband. That she assumes such authority could indicate that her husband has died, perhaps from starvation. It could also be the case that he has abandoned her. It is also possible that she is unwed with a child who was the product of prostitution. All of these circumstances would render her particularly defenseless. Widowhood in ancient Israel made one particularly vulnerable. Having no inheritance rights and being the subject of charity in wartime or famine would make for a precarious existence. If she never had a husband, her social standing as a mother would be even more diminished. She would be exposed to harsh treatment and exploitation.

The woman resides in Samaria, the capital of Israel, now under siege by the enemy, Aram. As a resident of this city, her life is conditioned by the social and cultural exigencies of the current political system. The story presumes a monarchic context. Elements within the tale, and within the larger surrounding narrative, sketch a monarchic framework and its accompanying ideology of domination and control. A monarchy presumes a hierarchically organized society. In the surrounding narrative recording the background of this northern kingdom, kings battle with other kings, leaving a trail of bloodshed. Power and privilege reside in the hands of a dominant royal class. The king, the sovereign in Israel, rules the nation and often vies with the prophet, the religious official. This hostility between prophets and kings characteristically erupted when the monarchial governance became abusive to its citizens. The prophets would condemn the social classism resulting from the ruler's policies, which could leave many citizens poor and landless. They also spoke out against the international conflicts that lead to warfare and apostasy.

Living within what were constructed to be the protective walls of Samaria, the woman—like other residents of the city—now is subject to the confinement that these walls and Ben-Hadad's surrounding army have secured (6:24). Hence, she is also subject to the economic conditions resulting from the siege. Because all supplies and foodstuffs coming into the capital city have been cut off, the woman, along with all the other citizens, are experiencing the effects of this blockade. How long and how serious is the famine to which she and other citizens are subjected?

A brief economic report offers a glance. An ass's head is selling in the marketplace for eighty shekels of silver. An ass was considered both a work animal as well as a common means of transportation. However, as an unclean animal, it did not typically serve as a food source. Yet a starving and besieged population understandably resorts to extreme measures. Desperate for anything that can sustain life, "even the most inedible part of an unclean animal becomes sustenance commanding a prince's ransom."[9] And the sale of one quarter of a qab of dove's dung was commanding fifty silver shekels. But how is such a commodity related to an understanding of famine resulting from the siege? A qab—a unit of measure—equals a little over a liter. Bird droppings often yield the whole undigested seeds that can be planted or even retrieved for human consumption. However, some scholars go so far as to insist upon the hyperbolic power of the statement. The siege was so prolonged, and thus the famine became so severe, that even "such filth as bird droppings were consumed by starving people and at a stiff price."[10] Hence, this graphic snippet of the day's market specials sketches a portrait of the dire circumstances that the woman and other residents of the city are experiencing. Further, that the most unsavory and unthinkable of provisions are now commanding such exorbitant prices in the market indicates that ordinary foods were no longer even available. Moreover, to even purchase these pathetic commodities required that one have the monetary means. Women caring for children without the means of a husband's support would be particularly helpless in such conditions.

The woman's location in the story world further confirms her exposed and endangered status in society. The first time she speaks in the narrative, she lifts up her voice to address Israel's king, who is walking on the wall surrounding the city. The hierarchical classism of the social order is made clear in this spatial description. While the king is walking on the top of the city wall, her implied social location is below, next to the wall. In ancient cities, the poor lived near or in the surrounding walls. Though no definitive mention is made of her economic or social standing, it is implied by what she reports. That she admits to engaging in cannibalism verifies that she has no means whatsoever of even purchasing what deplorable foodstuffs are available in the marketplace. And because there is no clear affiliation with a husband, whether due to widowhood, abandonment, or a status as unwed mother, the woman's standing in the community is marginal. Hence, that she happens to be at the wall and cries out to the king while he is walking on top of it, surveying the military crisis, suggests more than a coincidence. It is not difficult to imagine she lives near or in the wall, in the margins of the city, with the rest of the most impoverished of the population.

Likely unable to afford what little is available for purchase, the woman tells a story of how she is making ends meet in these ominous times. She and another mother have agreed to eat their children, and they have already eaten her son. Within the biblical tradition, cannibalism is well attested in times of military siege.[11] The Hebrew Scriptures cite parents eating their children in exceptionally grave circumstances (Deut 28:56-57; Lam 2:20, 4:10; Ezek.

5:10). Interpretations of these texts assume a clear link between lack of food in dire military straits and the resort to desperate measures as an explanation for this practice. Ample evidence from comparative literature, even if composed for propagandistic purposes, further reinforces the widespread and commonplace impression of cannibalism in the ancient Near East.[12] Hence, studies tend to contextualize cannibalism in such a way as to explain its presence in Israel and in the context of the Bible. However, it is significant to note that within Israelite tradition, the resort to cannibalism within the community recalls the curse in Deuteronomy (28:53-57). This Deuteronomic tradition, addressed in the second-person plural to the whole community, is also likely being echoed here. It warned that in wartime, men and women would eat the flesh of their offspring if Israel violated the covenant. But in this story, the portrait narrows, charging only a mother with the curse. How is it that this repugnant curse in Deuteronomy narrating fathers and mothers eating their children materializes only as this mother partaking in cannibalism? Perhaps, this woman so easily condemned for eating her child becomes a ready scapegoat representing both the iniquity of the community and its dreadful consequences. Further, a sociocultural exploration of cannibalism may confirm her status as victim of violence rather than its perpetrator.

On face value, the woman as the eater of her own child is reprehensible. As the doer of such violence, she is quickly and easily discounted as the victim. And though cannibalism is tied to the experience of famine in the story, the famine does not explain the cannibalism. Cannibalism is never just about eating or food stress. It is not merely a response to extreme hunger, as materialist theories have explained.[13] Many tribal and post tribal societies that hunger do not resort to cannibalism. Ecological and demographic factors that lead to famine, and hence to cannibalism in some societies, do not provoke this practice in others.[14]

Rather, cannibalism is a cultural practice, and it varies in meaning with each cultural context.[15] Being thus culturally constituted, it is laden with non-gustatory messages. While hunger is recognized as its motivation, hunger is secondary to larger concerns. Recent anthropological studies identify the overarching ethos of a cultural system as often standing in direct relationship to a community's response in times of food stress.[16] In societies where accommodation and integration with cosmic and social forces preside, notions of cannibalism are nonexistent. Harmony and integration prevail, particularly in the constructs of politics, government, and social order in these societies. Myths, rituals, and symbols tend to reflect these constructs and thus predicate and reinforce an abiding sociopolitical framework of tranquility and equality.[17]

By contrast, control and domination reign as the presiding mores in societies where cannibalism is practiced. The types of leadership, political structure, and social configuration in these societies express the prevailing constructs. Often these communities can claim a once-harmonious social order that has broken down. Reciprocal relations between persons and with nature have been replaced by hierarchized forms of governance. In some circumstances, cannibalism may be part of a hegemonic strategy developed in reaction to a perceived threat from natural or political forces. In other instances, it may be a response by those subject to or oppressed by controlling hierarchical forces in threatening circumstances.[18] Hence, cannibalism or its absence appears not to be the direct consequence of the scarcity of food but is specifically associated with the prevailing governing ethos of a society. Where accommodation and harmony are subordinate to or replaced by domination and control, cannibalism would be a more likely response to famine.[19]

Cannibalism as tied to hunger, therefore, is far more complex than simple cause and effect. Rather, its existence is yoked to a prevailing sociopolitical system of domination and control. The hunger for food that would motivate citizens to cannibalize coincides with sovereigns' voracious appetite for power and domination. The insatiable cravings of powerful inept rulers reign over the hunger of the powerless, who eventually resort to cannibalizing in the face of threat. The lives and destinies of powerless citizens, frequently women and children, too often become skeletal remains, left behind as the debris of the teeth-gnashing escapades of the powerful. As a consequence, the well-being and future of expendable persons are consumed and obliterated by the promotion of the livelihood and destiny of the privileged class. The fate of the powerless goes virtually unnoticed. The social framework that supports hegemonies of power and privilege effectively relegates these masses to the status of "other." In the case of this woman, her only identity, that of cannibal mother, makes her, at first glance, particularly objectionable and ensures her otherness.[20] The portrait of a woman as eater of her own child and willing to consume the child of another effectively obscures her status as a victim herself. Moreover, it tends to immunize most readers against the sympathies her plight might otherwise evoke. Her worth and delimited role as a complementary character is easily overshadowed by her own admission of cannibalism. Such an identification elicits shock, gasps, and rapt attention that curtail notice of the more gluttonous consumption of those who are responsible for the woman's horrific circumstances. Indeed, at first glance, this mother, who admits to cannibalizing a child, appears to be a doer of violence. But as we continue to probe her story, the analysis will reveal that this complementary character, as well as many other residents confined by this siege, are the real victims of violence whose lives are being consumed.

While the story provides examples from the economic and domestic sphere as to the conditions resulting from the famine, elaboration of such circumstances in the book of Lamentations offers further insights. The descriptions that detail conditions of starvation in Jerusalem during the final days of the Babylonian siege fill in the picture of conditions this desperate woman faces. Across five poems in Lamentations, lengthy and graphic depictions sketch the unimaginable consequences of food stress amidst military strife. The carcasses of children, once referred to as "the gold" or treasure of Israel, now lie strewn at the head of every street (Lam 4:1). That the tongues of thirsty, dying infants stick to the roofs of their mouths (4:4) suggests that their mothers' breasts have dried up and can no longer provide nourishment. Skin shriveled on bone has become dry as wood (4:8). And, significantly, Lamentations narrates that amidst these conditions of starvation, mothers boil and eat their children (4:10). More importantly, these mothers, who boil and eat their children, are referred to as "compassionate" (4:10). That cannibalizing mothers are described as compassionate catches the reader off guard. "Compassionate," a word derived from the Hebrew root רחם , meaning "womb," and used in the adjectival form, occurs elsewhere in the biblical tradition only with reference to God and divine activity (Exod 34:6; Deut 4:31; Joel 2:13; Jonah 4:2: Pss. 78:38, 86:1, 103:8, 111:4, 145:8; Neh 9:17, 31; 2 Chr 30:9). One can only conclude what we know of the ravages of international war: These conflicts and their consequences for innocent citizens on the ground change everything. So cannibalizing mothers are not horrific, but compassionate.[21] One Jerusalem resident cry in Lamentations offers clarification: "Happier are those pierced by the sword than those pierced by hunger, whose life drains away, deprived of the produce of the field" (4:9). The view here suggests a rapid death by an attacking sword is far preferable to the long, protracted experience of starvation (4:9). "Deprived of nourishment, one gradually becomes physically weak, mentally distraught, and spiritually depleted. It also requires that one cope with the growing awareness that life drains away due to starvation and that there is nothing that can be done to avert it."[22] Hence, Lamentations not only paints the painful portrait of human carnage in Jerusalem due to starvation but supplements the picture of Samaria under siege in our story.

Additionally, the depictions in Lamentations help to fill in the portrait of the woman in our account, coinciding with what is implied about her. While Lamentations provides unthinkable depictions of how starving people appear, our story omits any direct description of this starving woman. But the king's initial responses to her cry coincides with the descriptions in Lamentations and provides evidence of how she looks. When the king first responds to her initial summons, "Help, O King," he blames God for the famine, defining the winepress and the threshing floor as God's domain. Hence, his response suggests he knows from the woman's appearance about what she pleads before she even has a chance to explain. She appears as one suffering from starvation. Moreover, this mother's desperate account of her eating her own child confirms and further sketches her undescribed appearance—skeletal, groveling, and beseechingly desperate. What must be a woman with an emaciated, gaunt frame becomes even more lamentable when compared to the description of the king. Out of the utter lack of description of this woman, alongside the detail of the king's appearance, erupts an ironic contrast that provides even more disturbing information. The story not only narrates what the king is wearing on the outside, his royal robes. It also relates what he is wearing underneath, sackcloth. When the king tears his robes, he visibly displays sackcloth beneath his royal garments. The practice of wearing sackcloth, often subscribed to by kings in times of threatened disaster, is also accompanied by fasting in the Hebrew Scriptures (1 Kgs 21: 27; Jon 3:5, 8–9). Such penitence sought to curry divine favor in times of extreme crisis. But fasting makes sense only if one has access to food from which one abstains. So the economic violence that reigns down on citizens of Samaria due to kings and their conflicts reveals itself in the hypocrisy of a religious practice. While this starving woman resorts to eating her own child, due to a lack of food, the king is fasting from food evidently available to him.

When the woman speaks, her account discloses the domestic crisis wrought by the international crisis. Characteristic of a complementary character, this woman has an extended speaking part. In fact, she recites more words than anyone else in the tale. Yet her social position and the dynamics of power in this story make her voice all but inaudible. Even though she is the first to recite direct discourse, the narrative first features the privileged political parties in conflict, Ben-hadad and Israel's king. When she finally speaks, what she relates discloses the domestic crisis that this international power struggle has wrought. She details an agreement between herself and another mother to eat their children and even admits that they have already eaten her own child. Further, she reports that the other woman has now hidden her child and refuses to surrender him for food.

The woman's account of eating her child and her agreement with another woman is often interpreted as a summons for legal assistance. The woman is thought to be asking the king to exercise his authority and insist that the other mother make good on her word. However, it is unclear what the woman is requesting of the king. She may be beseeching the king to require the other mother to hand over her child for the day's food. Yet, such interchanges between kings and such subjects in wartime would be highly unlikely. [23] That a woman, who perhaps identifies with the margins of society and admits to eating her child, could persuade the king to act on her behalf is difficult to imagine. It is more plausible that she is setting before the king the kind of controversy that has erupted among citizens as an illustration of how desperate the siege situation has become. The woman addresses the king, sketching in graphic detail the unthinkable conditions resulting from the famine, as well as attesting to the disintegration of relationships that have resulted from its severity. As king, he is the only one who can do anything about this. Disregarding any breach of protocol designating who can speak or summon the king, she boldly and unapologetically cries out and witnesses to the desperation unfolding on the ground.

The contrast between her character and that of the king further thickens her portrait. Though powerless, the woman asserts initiative and, whether appropriate or not, speaks directly to the king. At this point, she apparently has nothing to lose. She is not interested in accusing him of failed responsibility toward citizens; rather, she pleads for him to do something about the ravaging conditions stemming from the political impasse over which he has control. By contrast, the king does not expend initiative to address the crisis. After hearing her story, he does not even address her directly or take responsibility for the crisis or even try to comfort her. Instead, he defends himself by engaging in the blame game. First, he points an accusing finger at God, declaring that God is in charge of the food sources. After he finally invites her to tell him what's wrong, he responds by transferring responsibility to the prophet Elisha and orders his beheading. So, now the king shifts blame to Elisha. Hence, this sovereign addresses the violence erupting from the prolonged siege by first blaming God, then blaming the prophet, and finally ordering more violence. Additionally, his vow to behead the prophet (6:31) turns attention away from the crisis of the starving woman and toward another power struggle in which he is engaged—the contest between king and the prophet. Thus, the story now turns to the prophet's house and concludes with a meeting between the king and the prophet.

Finally, the tension between the form and content of the story also does a disservice to the woman and relegates her character to the margins of the narrative. The priority of content in this account privileges the parties in conflict—Aram's king versus Israel's king, as well as Israel's king versus Elisha, the prophet. These characters, locked in hostile relations, open and close the story. But the priority of form centers upon the woman's tale.

6:24	Ben Hadad and his army	Authorities in a struggle for power
6:26	Israel's king walking on the wall of the city	
6:27–29	The woman and her story	Starving woman struggling to live
6:30	Israel's king walking on the wall of the city	Authorities in a struggle for power
6:31–33	The prophet and the elders in his house	

This chiastic framework constructs the narrative so that the woman's story is the poetic centerpiece. Yet, as the tale unfolds, she is not center-staged. The magnitude of the national and international struggles for power that surround her dwarf the centrality of this woman's story in the poetics of the tale. The larger story of kings and prophets minimizes the account of this mother's implied tale of starvation and the struggle for food. Sandwiched between these political contestants vying for domination and control, this woman and her story, along with the whole city's starving population, are being swallowed up by the struggles of the privileged in the narrative and powerful in the society. Hence, this complementary character summons our attention and requires that we recognize how the construction of stories can feature some characters in ways that distract us from crucial lessons that supporting cast characters have to offer.

CONCLUSION

Ignoring the story of this complementary character not only requires participation in the caste system of the narrative, it also risks missing the important lessons about violence that her character discloses. While the woman's own story sets forth an immediate and urgent crisis, it warrants no resolution in the tale. Its outcome remains unknown. As the story progresses, the conflict between those in power—kings and prophets—remains at the forefront and quickly overshadows this woman's fate. Failing to recognize such violence cultivates complicity with violence. As we acclimate to reading past accounts of it in the text, we are more likely to walk past instances of it in our world. And therein reside the consequences. Complicity with violence enables violence to increase and have its way. The descriptions of violence as labyrinth-like or even "amazing" are apt. "The paths that seem to exit from the madness of violence so often lead deeper into its maze."[24]

While the woman's account sets forth circumstances that are urgent and life-threatening, her narrative warrants no resolution. Its outcome remains unknown. As the story unfolds, the conflict between those in power—the kings and the prophet—remains at the forefront and quickly overrides the woman's dilemma. But the woman represents more than herself. Her story relates much more than the crisis of her own life. She signifies all those whose life plans, identity, significance, and well-being are overshadowed and consumed by the insatiable cravings and jockeying for power of political and religious leaders in the text and in our world. These contests lead to war, the mechanisms of which include blockades of supplies, incineration of whole villages, taking of hostages, sieges of cities, executions, and so on. The often unseen consequences—displacement of whole populations, famine, lifelong trauma, widespread disease, massive loss of life, youth deprived of futures—all reap unimaginable consequences for multitudes of anonymous victims.

War in all its manifestations redefines everything. It disrupts the most fundamental dynamism, that is, relationships, that makes one human. "Indeed, a mother whose maternal instinct has failed symbolizes a world in chaos."[25] But her cannibalism serves as more than merely the exponent of the moral depravity of a society gone awry. At first encounter, what seems like an appalling story of a woman eating her child to save herself, actually discloses a woman who is not heartless or selfish. Rather, she represents the utter desperation in the face of starvation resulting from unaddressed political strife, which has reaped a prolonged and profound famine. Consuming her own flesh and blood, she sacrifices her own destiny. Surrendering her maternal instinct, she becomes alienated from the only role that defines her in that society. But this capitulation to the pangs of starvation and the violence all around should not indict her. She and her child are the expiatory offering, bearing the iniquities of a self-serving and corrupt political system that takes care of itself rather than its citizens. Caught up in the horror of a torturous time, her life has become unimaginably altered by war, loss, famine, and a child who likely had already perished before she ever consumed him.

> The pathos of choice on how to proceed in wartime, how to live in the misery of defeat, how to survive your own child's death as you yourself slowly starve to death sets forth an excruciating example of the depths of human suffering. The ravages of war then and today comprehensively redefine everything—survival, motherhood, and even compassion.[26]

How we read this text does matter. As we see and ask questions in these texts, so we see and make inquiries in our world. We can glance at or look past those anonymous others, who seem to be the doers of violence, and level a quick and uncritical judgment. Or we can take a prolonged look at many of these individuals. In the process, we might discover that often those anonymous others, so easily indicted for doing violence, are actually the victims of long-standing systemic social and political violence themselves. Therefore, they do not deserve an indicting rejection and a hasty judgment. Taken seriously, their cry from below, like that of this woman, summons us for a response that can lift them up, restore their humanity, and confirm their worth.

NOTES

1. See Gina Hens-Piazza, *Nameless, Blameless and Without Shame—Two Cannibal Mothers Before a King* (Collegeville, MN: Liturgical Press, 2003) that sets forth a full length feminist analysis of this story illustrating a postmodern approach.
2. Numerous proposals have been made for the translation and understanding of an ass's head and dove's dung as food items. See Gwilym Jones, *1 and 2 Kings*, vol. 2, New Century Bible Commentary (Grand Rapids, MI: Eerdmans, 1984), 431–32, for a summary of these proposals.
3. Some scholars argue that the woman's appeal, "Help, O King," is a legal address requesting the king's judicial arbitration. See Mordechai Cogan and Hayim Tadmor, *II Kings*,

Anchor Bible Commentary (New York: Doubleday, 1988), 79; Stuart Lasine, "Jehoram and the Cannibal Mothers (2 Kings 6.24–33): Solomon's Judgment in an Inverted World," *Journal for the Study of the Old Testament* 50 (1991): 48; and James Montgomery and Henry Gehman, *The Books of Kings*, International Critical Commentary (New York: Scribner, 1957), 385. However, the king's initial response in 6:27 does not indicate that he necessarily understands her salutation as a legal request.

4. The majority of translations argue in favor of reading "the king" (*hammelek*) for the Masoretic Text's "the messenger" (*hammal'ak*) in v. 33

5. Lasine, "Jehoram and the Cannibal Mothers," 32–33.

6. Richard Nelson, *First and Second Kings,* Interpretation Commentary (Atlanta, GA: John Knox, 1987), 189.

7. Robert LaBarbera, "The Man of War and the Man of God: Social Satire in 2 Kings 6:8-7:20," *Catholic Biblical Quarterly* 46 (1984): 646–47.

8. See Walter Brueggemann, *2 Kings,* Knox Preaching Guides (Atlanta: John Knox, 1982), 25-26, who argues that while "the ostensible problem is famine . . . the center of interest to be stressed in preaching is the exchange between king and prophet."

9. Robert Alter, *Ancient Israel: The Former Prophets: Joshua, Judges, Samuel, Kings: A Translation with Commentary* (New York: W. W. Norton & Company, 2014), 729 n.25.

10. Ibid.

11. See Jonas Greenfield, *Storia e tradizioni di Israele* (Brescia, Italy: Paideia Editrice, 1991), 125; Gray, 523; Jones, 433; Montgomery and Gehman, 385; Wiseman, 211; Cogan and Tadmor, 80.

12. Josephus' record of the practice at the time of the Roman siege of Jerusalem (*Bellum Judaicum* 6.3.4) and the instances of cannibalism during Ashurbanipal's siege of Babylon (Luchenbill, *Records II*, 190; Oppenheim, *Iraq* 17, 69f) are often cited. See Jones, 433; Wiseman, 211; Cogan and Tadmor, 80; Montgomery and Gehman, 385; and Gray, 523.

13. For example, see Michael Harner, "The Ecological Basis for Aztec Sacrifice," *American Ethnologist* 4 (1979): 17–35; and Marvin Harris, *Cannibals and Kings: The Origins of Cultures* (New York: Random House, 1977), who propose hunger and protein deficiency as explanations for human sacrifice among the Aztecs.

14. The sociocultural exposition on cannibalism that follows first appeared in a feminist interpretation of this text. See Gina Hens-Piazza, "Forms of Violence and the Violence of Forms: Two Cannibal Mothers before a King (2 Kings 6:24–33)," *Journal of Feminist Studies in Religion* 14 (1998): 91–104.

15. For a study of the practice and significance of cannibalism as related to particular cultures, see the collection of essays in Pamela Brown and Don Tuzin, eds., *The Ethnography of Cannibalism* (Washington, DC: Society for Psychological Anthropology, 1983).

16. For an extended study of cannibalism as tied to the prevailing ethos of a cultural system, see Peggy Reeves Sanday, *Divine Hunger: Cannibalism as a Cultural System* (Cambridge, UK: Cambridge University Press, 1986).

17. For example, the Mbutis of the Ituri Forest in northeastern Congo are guided by a worldview that is antithetical to the governing strategies and social configuration of domination, mastery, and control over nature. Each individual is imbued with a life force derivative of a larger source, embodied by the forest on which his or her life depends. Harmony with the forces of nature, as embodied in nature and in each individual, is essential to the well-being of the society. Physical violence, as a response to famine or as a means of resolving a dispute, would be tantamount to sacrilege. When faced with the prospect of enduring famine, the Mbutis believe the order and harmony have been disrupted and require reinstatement. For example, when hunting and fishing fail, the Mbutis conduct a ceremony that addresses potential oppositions within the community—between male and female, chaos and order, and forest and camp. This ethos of harmony and integration in the wake of an absence of food among other comparable societies, such as the Navajo and the people of Ik, also coincides with an absence of cannibalism. See ibid., 214–31.

18. The social and political order of both the Aztecs and the Iroquois (especially the Huron) was constituted in terms of struggle and control. Cannibalism and sacrifice were primordial metaphors that symbolized domination and submission, the ethos of these societies. The magni-

tude of the sacrifice and torture complex associated with cannibalism increased sharply in response to drought, famine, and competition among Native American groups in the face of European expansion. See ibid., 125–50; and Marshall Sahlins, "Culture as Protein and Profit," *New York Review of Books,* 25 (1978): 45–53.

19. Sanday, 54–55.

20. Reading colonial and postcolonial literature and its appropriation has shaped my understanding of the parallels between this woman subject and other subjects colonized by various kinds of political, social and cultural domination, all of whom are easily relegated to the position of "other." The second edition of the collection of essays in Bill Ashcroft, Gareth Griffiths, and Helen Tiffin, eds., *The Post-Colonial Reader* (London: Routledge, 2004) provides an excellent introduction.

21. Instead, Phyllis Trible, *God and the Rhetoric of Sexuality,* Overtures to Biblical Theology (Philadelphia: Fortress Press, 1978), 33, suggests that these women were formerly compassionate but have lost their capacity to feel compassion.

22. Gina Hens-Piazza, *Lamentations: Wisdom Commentary,* vol. 30 (Collegeville, MN: Liturgical Press, 2017), 65.

23. The story of Solomon and the two mothers is the other parallel instance where women from a lower social class are portrayed as directly addressing the king (1 Kgs 3:15–28). However, their crisis is not related to a condition stemming from war or military siege. And while tradition has often portrayed this story as an example of Solomon's wisdom, recent studies read the account as a critique of his kingship. One scholar, who reads these two stories together, observes that "2 Kings 6:24–33 may actually be Solomon's world with the skin off, so to speak, a world where the assumptions and pretensions of kings are shown up for what they are—a world where Solomon's unbending harshness, epitomized in his willingness to divide the child, has led to the division of his kingdom under his son Rehoboam, whose weak attempts at bullying tactics are a parody in themselves of his father's strength." See Hugh Pyper, "Judging the Wisdom of Solomon: The Two-Way Effect of Intertextuality," *Journal of the Study of the Old Testament 59* (1993): 34.

24. Gil Bailie, *Violence Unveiled: Humanity at the Crossroads* (New York: Crossroads, 1995), 89.

25. Claudia Camp, "1 and 2 Kings," in *The Women's Bible Commentary*, 3rd edition, eds., Carol Newsom and Sharon Ringe (Louisville, KY: Westminster John Knox, 1992), 108.

26. Mary Olowin, "The Pathos of Choice," in *Lamentations: Wisdom Commentary*, 66–67.

Chapter Four

Unsung Courage and Fidelity

A Study of Bit-Part Characters in 2 Kings 5:1–19

Among the supporting cast resides a second group of characters who are designated as playing "bit parts" in the organizational scheme of this study. The term, "bit parts," stems from formal labels indicating characters' roles in drama. Indeed, the supporting cast members of this group in biblical texts do share some of the defining features of those in plays and theater. For example, characters in the Bible, like actors in drama who play bit parts, have a very limited number of lines to recite. They also both interact with the principal actor or protagonist directly or wield a significant influence on him or her indirectly by their speech or actions. Also, both groups usually appear and disappear rather quickly on the set or in the story. However, the identification of other similarities stops here. In drama, bit part actors, often referred to as "extras," suggests that they are dispensable and mere functionaries. The dictionary definition of them in drama renders them "a small or unimportant part in a play or drama."[1] Such characterization implies that they lack complexity and discourages attending to their importance or necessity in the story.

By contrast, bit-part characters in this taxonomy of the supporting cast in the Bible are quite significant. Despite their abbreviated appearance in the story, they often play a pivotal role. Unlike their counterparts, defined by the limits of their theater definitions, bit-part characters in the Bible are present by means of both narrated discourse and direct discourse.[2] Often their entry to the story is preceded by some brief introduction or even description. Following, they have a featured speaking part. Moreover, what they say, how they speak, and to whom their words are addressed often become a further means by which we know them. Their speech, and sometimes the action they take during their very truncated appearance in the story, often prompt another character to act or to change. Their brief presence may instigate a new direction for the plot or even have a direct hand in the resolution of the crisis or problem that unfolds across a tale.

Bit-part biblical characters actually share many of the characteristics of the first group, the complementary characters. However, the key distinguishing feature between the two groups is largely one of quantity. Bit-part characters, like complementary characters, have staying power in the narrative, but it is of a more subtle nature or often an indirect impact. In addition, their direct speech assumes significance and can alter the course of the story, but it is much more limited. Like complementary characters, they may even bear significance in highlighting a key theme or motif of the story. But again, their influence in this regard will be less direct or more curtailed. Finally, this study assumes that each story speaks of many stories. And every character has a story embedded in the narrative. Complementary characters often have their story intertwined with the story unfolding in the narrative. It is definable and may function as a subplot, so to speak, that can be constructed by what the narrative relates about them and the role they play by their speech and actions in the plot. Bit parts characters' also have their own story to tell; but because they are almost always anonymous and afforded much less air time and narrative description, their story is often implied. Thus, it needs to be deduced from the clues inscribed in their brief descriptions or from the few lines they recite. It might even be informed with reference to their counterparts in other stories about whom more detail is afforded. Hence, the study of bit-part characters in the Bible enjoins the reader's effort to a greater degree than complementary characters. Yet, the yield often exceeds expectations and offers unexpected insights that we don't want to miss.

AN EXAMPLE: 2 KINGS 5:1–19[3]

Traditionally, 2 Kgs 5:1–14 is characterized with reference to two of its main characters: Naaman, a Syrian general, and Elisha, Israel's prophet. It is the first of three acts (vv. 1–14, 15–19, 20–27), each comprising a self-contained story that narrates the conditions out of which the subsequent act develops. Each of the three acts spotlights one of three main characters—Naaman, Elisha, and Gehazi, a servant of Elisha, respectively. All are depicted with particular depth and detail. Their vividness not only makes them front and center in the narrative, it also subtly downplays or even obscures any other characters present in the tale.

Act one (vv. 1–14), the primary focus of this study, introduces Naaman in a most extended way. He serves as a military officer of Aram, one of Israel's archenemies. He enjoys not only the favor of Aram's king, but unbeknownst to Naaman, he himself is also regarded by Israel's God, who has granted him victory over Israel itself (v. 1). But all this greatness is qualified by an addendum to his notoriety. Naaman is afflicted with a skin disease,[4] which helps shift the focus to the figure of Elisha. While never appearing on the set in this first act, Elisha brings about a cure for the Syrian general. Moreover, the prophet's program sets the stage for Naaman's spiritual healing, which will be taken up in the second act.

In part two of the drama (vv. 15–19), Naaman, who has been physically healed of his skin disease, undergoes a spiritual metamorphosis. Standing before the prophet Elisha, Naaman first confesses his faith in Israel's God; he also acknowledges that this God is the only God in all the world (v. 15). In the third and concluding scene (vv. 20–27), Gehazi second-guesses Elisha's decision to refuse payment from Naaman. He crafts a deceptive ploy to gain those gifts Naaman had offered Elisha. As punishment, Gehazi becomes afflicted with a skin disease. Hence, the conclusion of the third act returns thematically to the opening of the first act. The exploitative Gehazi ends up afflicted with the same condition from which Naaman miraculously is cleansed.

Commentaries seize upon this reversal as the heart of the story's lesson.[5] Naaman's conversion and profession of faith challenge any notions of exclusivity on the part of Israel's God.[6] Like the books of Ruth and Jonah, the story of Naaman tells of a foreigner's witness to the one true God.[7] Naaman's gratitude for his cure from a skin disease stands in sharp contrast to Gehazi's greed, which results in his affliction.[8] Other studies focus upon the characters of Elisha and Naaman, exploring the lessons that this duo prompts.[9] In this light, connections are readily made between this miracle story and Jesus's healing of a leper. Again and again, the lessons and interpretive insights derived from this story stem from the interactions of these three characters.

In contrast, rich interpretive yield can be harvested by fixing attention upon members of the supporting cast resident in the story, whose presence and influence in the narrative are easily missed or disregarded. Confining the focus to the first act (vv. 1–14), the presence of several influential characters are notable. Two kings play a brief role here. Given their history of hostilities, the cameo appearances by the king of Aram and the king of Israel (likely Jehoram) add to the narrative tension. Naaman's wife plays an implied role in his decision to seek a cure in Israel. Elisha's brotherhood of prophets, gathered in his home, and the messenger that Elisha sends out to speak with Naaman assume importance in the development of the plot.

Two other thinly sketched, but noteworthy, characters enter the narrative in this first act playing bit parts. In the opening of the story, a servant girl informs Naaman's wife about the prospect of a healing in Israel for the military general (vv. 2–3). Midway into Naaman's pursuit of that healing, his own servants rescue the indignant general from what might have become a disastrous about-face (v. 13). Interspersed at strategic points throughout the narrative, the servant girl and these servants are easily discounted by the caste system of our literary categories. They are labeled as mere "agents," simply existing to move the story forward.[10] Their designation as "servants" further effaces any particularity or interest that their presence might generate. They are servants in the content of the story, and they serve as literary props in the story's analysis. Grounded primarily in a labor theory of character,[11] commentaries often treat them as subsidiary or ignore them altogether. They are what might be called the collective subaltern of the narrative.

Determined to offer a more democratized reading, this analysis turns its attention away from Naaman and Elisha and instead toward the servant figures in 2 Kgs 5:1–14. It recognizes that at first glance, these servants qualify as mere literary props, according to traditional literary analysis and its categories of importance. As bit-part characters, they do have a story to tell, though it is not readily featured. But characteristic of this particular group of supporting cast players, if the reader attends closely to the reduced narrative space these servants do occupy and listens attentively to what few lines they are assigned to recite, a great deal about them begins to emerge. For even though the servant girl and Naaman's servants appear briefly in the narrative, recite their lines, and then quickly disappear from the account, their symbolic and thematic value endures in the culmination of the story's conclusion. Hence, taking these characters seriously may persuade readers to grant them far more importance than they have received in the past. Moreover, we might even discover that these servants, though most marginalized and least among the characters of this narrative, are in fact the greatest.

THE SERVANT GIRL

The story of the servant girl (vv. 2–4) begins and ends at the opening of the Naaman story. Her appearance is brief, a mere three verses. Only two verses (vv. 2–3) are directly focused upon her and the part she plays in this tale (vv. 1–14). The third time she is mentioned, the notation is secondary; the narrator focuses instead upon the chain of communication that indirectly reports her plan to the king and references only that she is the speaker (v. 4). Consistent with her role as "servant" in her master's house and her minor importance in the narrator's view, she is not the subject but the object in the sentence when introduced in the tale (v. 2). Yet, a great deal can be inferred about her. She is more than just a servant girl. We learn that she is young and an Israelite (v. 2). Readers can glean from the context of the story that she may have been a captive of war, possibly the war in which Naaman—as head of Aram's forces—was victorious over Israel. This was the war where Yahweh granted Aram victory over the Israelites (v. 1). However, unbeknownst to Naaman, the outcome of the battle that may have occasioned this servant girl's presence in Naaman's life will qualify the victory as more than just a "military" feat. Her presence will not only grant Naaman emancipation from his a skin disease, but will ultimately afford him much more.[12]

The initial description of the young servant girl forms a telling contrast with the preceding introduction of Naaman that opens the story. He is the great Syrian conqueror; she is the little Israelite captive. He is the male adult authority; she is the female young servant. And, while we know Naaman's name and his high rank, she, as a bit-part character, remains anonymous and without status.[13] Yet, one other difference catches the attention of the close reader and hints at the drama about to unfold. Though fashioned in unqualified renown, Naaman's greatness is qualified. He has a skin disease.[14] By contrast, the description of the servant girl offers no qualification of her personal well-being.

As we probe the narrative, details emerge that could jeopardize any quality of life for this young girl. Because she is a prisoner of war, we can surmise that she "was before the wife of Naaman" (v. 2)[15] in the role of servant, likely against her own wishes.[16] Denied freedom, she has been taken from her own country as war booty. It is logical then to conclude that she was, early in life, cut off from her family, friends, home, and all that was familiar to her. That "bands from Aram had gone out and taken captive" (v. 2) this young girl suggests the trauma of her transport.[17] This young Israelite girl was carried away by foreign soldiers. We know nothing about the story of her journey in the company of enemy troops. But it is not difficult to imagine the fear and anxiety that might plague her as a result of such an ordeal.

Despite the brief description she is accorded, closer reading reveals much that is implied about her character. Though young and a foreigner, she does not lack initiative. And while her brief appearance might deem her characterization insignificant, she recites the first direct speech of the story. Soon after the problem of Naaman's a skin disease is introduced, she—and only she—addresses it. The young girl informs Naaman's wife of the prospect for a cure in Israel. Using the language of condition, this young captive informs the general's wife that "*if only* my master (Naaman) was *before* the prophet who is in Samaria, *then* he (the prophet) would cure him of his a skin disease" (v. 3). With an economy of words, the nameless servant youth sets forth the prospect of a somewhat miraculous healing for the great military leader. There is cause and effect embedded in her recitation. Naaman must play a part in procuring his healing so that the prophet can restore him. The "if . . . then" construction indicates that the healing is premised upon condition. "If only" he presents himself before the prophet in Samaria, "then" he will be healed.

Two particulars of the servant girl's statement reveal yet more about her character. First, the "if" language of her recital conveys her conviction about one's responsibility when it comes to being healed. One has to act—to do what is required. Healing in Israel has terms attached to it. But the conditional "if" of her proposal is softened by her addition of "only." Her words, "If only," convey not only the requirement, but also her desire that he carry out the requirement. They subtly convey her hope that he will do what is needed so he can be restored.[18] With the enticing rhetoric of "if only," she plants a seed about the possibility of a different future for Naaman. What she envisions levels a challenge to her master to make a decision. He can continue in his infirmed state and remain in Aram. Or, on the premise of the girl's proposal, he can present himself before the prophet in Samaria. The servant's language not only defines the stipulation of the venture; it also expresses the outcome of such a jaunt to Samaria. "Then he (the prophet) would cure him of his a skin disease" (v. 3). The outcome of the girl's vision suggests her optimism and faith. The future holds the potential for a renewed existence for the general. Her proposal expresses the idealism of a youth who believes, against all odds, that healing for an Aramaen general can come about before an Israelite prophet.

Second, in this servant girl's only oration, her choice of words specifies yet another condition of the healing with the term *before*. Naaman needs to present himself *before* the prophet in Samaria. The word *before* (Hebrew = *lipně*) is frequently used in Hebrew to designate the status of one who is in the service of or pays allegiance "before" another.[19] When introduced in the story, Naaman is identified as "a great man *before* his lord" (v. 1), characterizing his service and allegiance to Aram's king. Immediately following, the servant girl is identified as the young girl from Israel who is "*before* the wife of Naaman" (v. 2), indicating her status as a household servant. Now, again, the servant girl's proposal uses the language of allegiance. Naaman must present himself "*before* the prophet who is in Samaria." Because the introduction portrays Naaman as the great military general in Aram (v. 1) who already pays allegiance and fidelity before his king (v. 1), the condition of the servant girl's proposal is problematic. Naaman, who acts on her initiative, is evidently persuaded by her overture, but by only part of what she says. Convinced that the goal set forth by the servant girl—namely, a healing—is available in Israel, Naaman makes plans for the journey. However, this great military general will not conform to the means that she proposes. He has his own ideas about how he will achieve the outcome. Indeed, he will travel to Israel. But Naaman's actions indicate he has no plans to present himself before anyone. Instead, Naaman revises her plan in order to avoid placing himself in a compromised position *before* any other authority, especially an Israelite king or prophet.

Skipping over the communication of the servant girl's proposal from Naaman's wife to Naaman, and from Naaman to the king, the narrative swiftly redefines the protocol by which this a skin disease will be cured. First, Aram's king, who has recently been victorious over Israel, will write a letter to Israel's king concerning the business surrounding Naaman's visit. Hence, this will be strictly a political negotiation. In no way will Naaman present himself *before* Israel's king or, as the servant girl proposed, "before the prophet in Samaria" (v. 3). Aram's king will continue to be the only one before whom Naaman stands and pays allegiance. Second, the service of a healing will leave no obligation on the part of Aram's general, Naaman; he will journey to Israel amply prepared to pay for the healing. With economic means of "ten talents of silver, six thousand shekels of gold and ten sets of clothing," (v. 5) and the political capital of a letter from Aram's king (v. 6), a new scheme replaces the servant girl's proposed condition.

What Naaman packs along for the trade is indeed sizable. In the Old Testament, a talent and a shekel were both units of weight. A talent was equivalent to 75 pounds, and a shekel equaled approximately .4 ounces. Therefore, Naaman brings with him approximately 750 pounds of silver and 150 pounds of gold. The ten sets of clothing are also of high value. Sets of garments were the customary gift or payment of great men. They were signs of status and wealth.[20] Loaded down with loot, Naaman intends to purchase the healing service rather than present himself in some subservient position before the prophet in Samaria. In order to ensure that his greatness and status as military general remain intact when he departs, he carts along a load of weighty collateral. The contrast between the servant girl's idea and Naaman's own vision of how this healing will occur is stark. The servant girl says nothing about a gift, an offering or a payment. Her suggestion sketches an unencumbered, empty-handed image of Naaman before the prophet. Naaman instead loads up his chariot with goods and capital in anticipation of a goods-for-service transaction.

The proposal of the young girl and the plan actually hatched by Naaman and his king reveal a great deal about their contrasting characters. The servant girl's wish for Naaman gives witness to her priorities—her deep religious conviction and faith in the prophet and his God. By contrast, Naaman's revised scheme testifies to what he most values—nationalism and egotism. Armed with a demanding letter from his king and a chariot full of goods, Naaman transforms the young servant's faith-based proposal into an economic and political transaction. Hence, while the word of the servant girl determines where Naaman will go, it does not dictate what he will do. In keeping with their vastly different social positions, he will readily make use of her ideas but will certainly not do as she proposes. Still, in the broader story world, the initiative of this bit-part character, portrayed as a young prisoner of war, sets in motion not only Naaman's fate, but also the story's more extended plotline, which ultimately unfolds beyond either of their plans.

Though the healing that could come to Naaman is praiseworthy, the servant girl's suggestion is risky. That Israel and Aram are archenemies makes her suggestion precarious, if not suspect. What could be the consequence for her if he is refused a cure? What if his effort to procure a healing fails? What if a public outcry arises against him for even being in Samaria, Israel's capital? Naaman's seeking a remedy in Israel could be degrading or even dangerous to the powerful military general.

In contrast to Aram, where one with a skin disease could rise to the status of a great military general, persons in Israel afflicted with such a condition were regarded as impure. Such a condition often rendered one an outcast.[21] The "great military general," who enjoyed high regard in Aram, might suffer public humiliation in Israel's capital. The consequences for a foreigner like Naaman to show up in Israel with such an affliction are potentially grave.

As we ponder all that the servant girl's actions imply, the question of her character's credibility inevitably arises. Why would this servant girl subject herself to the repercussions that would almost certainly rain down upon her if Naaman were scorned or humiliated in her country? If one can rise to the status of the top military leader in Aram with a skin disease, why does she even bother to make the suggestion about a healing? Does she sense his feeling of being incomplete or unfulfilled because of this infirmity? Does she, as an outsider of marginal status, perceive that he feels marginalized or qualified about his own worth on account of his skin disease? Or does she understand that a healing from Yahweh's prophet might challenge Naaman in places where he needs healing most?

Certainly, the most basic question is, who is this servant child? Can we prod the narrative for more insights that her character reveals? Perhaps what emerges first is the unshakable confidence she presumably has in the prophet. Prophets during the early united monarchy played roles as intermediaries between the king and Israel's God.[22] Nathan advises David as to his sin and what will result because of his deed. He also instructs Bathsheba, David's wife, in how to facilitate the rise of her son Solomon to kingship. After the division of the kingdom, prophets continued in their roles as intermediaries. However, as kings ran amok, many of the prophets turned their attention to facilitating a relationship between God and the people.[23]

Elisha is the prophet in Samaria about whom the servant girl speaks. While Samaria was established as a capital under the Omride dynasty, the whole territory of Israel is often referred to as Samaria. Given Elisha's narrated activities, it is likely that the servant girl intended Naaman to encounter the prophet somewhere in the Samarian countryside, not necessarily the capital city. Following in the tradition of Elijah, much of Elisha's prophetic activities were fixed upon intermediating on behalf of the people.[24] He acts on behalf of a widow and her children (2 Kgs 4:1–7), he purifies the deadly waters of a town's people (2 Kgs 2:19–22), and he restores life to the Shunammite woman's child (2 Kgs 4:18–37). Caught up in even more mundane activities of the Israelite people's lives, he rescues an ax from the water (2 Kgs 6:1–7), purifies a pot of bad stew (2 Kgs 4: 38–41), and feeds a hungry crowd (2 Kgs 4:42–44). Hence, the servant girl is proposing not only that Naaman present himself before the prophet in Samaria, but that he present himself before a prophet who is not so much identified with the king but rather with the common people.[25] For the great military general who does not even acknowledge Israel's God and certainly does not think of himself as among the common people, such a condition must have seemed unconscionable to Naaman.

That the servant girl's confidence extends beyond the prophet can also be detected here. As channel for divine favors and miracles, the prophet was specifically identified with Israel's God. Seeking the prophet's assistance presumed one's faith in this deity. The risks incurred by this servant girl's proposal likely are premised, not only on her belief in the prophet, but more particularly on her well-grounded faith in God.

The faith of the servant girl is further illuminated by contrast with that of another character. Naaman heads to Israel and presents the letter sent by his king to the ruler in Samaria. The surrounding narrative helps identify this king as Jehoram, the last successor of the Omride dynasty to reign in Israel. The letter indicates the purpose of Naaman's visit—namely, to be cured. When King Jehoram reads the letter, he tears his garments. Tearing of royal robes, of which this king seems to have a habit (2 Kgs 6:24), can signify one's despair or repentance in the current circumstances. The king's speech makes clear what the ripping of his robes means here. Consistent with his usual approach to crisis,[26] he expresses despair, claims a complete inability to address the problem because he is not God, and defines the request for a healing as a ploy on the part of Aram's ruler to "pick a fight with him" (v. 7). Furthermore, the king gives no indication of knowledge that healing is even available in his land. Whether he lacks this knowledge or refuses to acknowledge Elisha's activities remains uncertain. That this king and Elisha had tense relations is narrated consistently in the surrounding traditions (2 Kgs 3:13–14; 6:2–3). Perhaps given his less than amicable relation with the prophet, the king would rather surrender to despair before this foreign general than stoop to acknowledge the religious power of Elisha, who has continually challenged him. His recognition of the prophet's potential to assist would require acknowledgement on the king's part of a power other than his own authority. It would require, at least, an initial gesture of faith in the prophet's healing abilities.

By contrast, the Israelite servant girl, who is powerless and far away in Aram, expresses complete confidence and faith that healing for the general is possible in her land before the prophet. Though both she and Israel's king are confronted with the same problem, Naaman's skin disease, they respond in completely opposite ways. She immediately envisions a solution, detailing where and how a cure can take place. Israel's king, on the other hand, throws up his hands in hopelessness and redefines Naaman's request as an antagonistic overture.

Having considered some of the details of her description, the elements of her proposal, and the issues embedded in her own story, the young servant girl's role, though brief, now appears quite significant. In the midst of an account riveted upon the great army general Naaman, the hostile and powerful kings of Aram and Israel, and the miracle working prophet Elisha, this servant girl, playing but a bit part, begins to emerge as one of the most compelling figures of all.

As we read with admiration of this young servant's brave overture in what were apparently hostile circumstances, we become aware that the theme of inclusivity extends beyond what most interpretations assign this passage.[27] That Naaman, the foreign general, is cured by Israel's prophet and comes to believe in Israel's God is thought to challenge misunderstandings about Israel's electedness. Now this young girl's initiative and faith require broadening those boundaries of inclusivity to accommodate servants, females, and youth.[28] Through her audacious action, this servant child exposes such social divisions as mere facades and challenges us not only to rethink who are the real heroes in this tale. She ultimately nudges us to reconsider who are the real heroes in our world.

Like bit-part characters, even when the young girl servant disappears from the story, resonances of her character and influence persist. When Naaman is finally cured (v. 14), the description—"his flesh was restored like the flesh of a young boy"—clarifies the reversal of his encumbered state.[29] Indeed, the great military general is healed. But when Naaman's a skin disease is resolved, the description of his healed flesh reveals yet more. The language "like that of a young boy" (*qaton naar*) parallels the initial description of the young servant girl (*qatonah naarah*) (v. 2).[30] In the opening of the story, the description of Naaman and the characterization of the servant girl emphasize their differences. In his healed state at the conclusion, Naaman is described in a manner that forges a new bond between them. Further, because he is healed, Naaman is about to embark on another, deeper journey. A member of the supporting cast, this young girl servant, who had great faith, foreshadows the great officer, who is now himself on the road to faith.

OTHER SERVANTS

We return now to the larger narrative in order to give scrutiny to other members of the supporting cast who also play bit parts. When Naaman arrives in Samaria and presents Israel's king with a letter, other servants enter the story. Again, in resisting the narrator's focus, we encounter members of the supporting cast whose skill and wisdom deserve elaboration and study. Word of the arrival of Aram's military general in Samaria and the letter sent by Aram's king has evidently spread. The narrative skips over a direct communication to the prophet of this news. Instead, we hear only that Elisha responds and, once again, has rescued Israel's king from his characteristic pessimism and habit of assigning blame. The first time we hear Elisha speak, he questions Jehoram's reaction and then commands the king to send Naaman to him. The account bypasses the report of the Syrian general's journey to Elisha and immediately describes Naaman's arrival at the prophet's house. The narrative specifies that Naaman pulls up with horses and his chariot (v. 9). Such an extravagant entourage implies that Naaman is not traveling alone. A military general traveling so far and loaded down with costly goods would surely not arrive unattended. However, there is no mention of the other characters accompanying him until it is time for them to provide a service for Naaman.

Recall that Naaman had planned to avoid any subservient position before the prophet. However, his plan is undercut by the prophet's actions. Elisha never even comes out to face the general or to speak to him. Instead, he sends a messenger with a directive for Naaman. Without greeting, salutation, or explanation, the emissary of the prophet reports Elisha's directive to this Syrian official. With two grammatical imperatives, Naaman is commanded to "*go* and *wash* yourself seven times in the Jordan and your flesh will be restored and you will be cleansed" (v. 10).

Using the language of authority, the prophet commands the Aramean general in what he must do. Naaman, who is accustomed to giving orders himself, is now being ordered. He has to wash himself not once but seven times in the Jordan, the largest and most important river in Palestine. This body of water, running north to south, registers as the natural lifeline of the nation of Israel. While disputed, the name Jordan likely derives from Semitic origin, with the root meaning "to go down."[31] So, in addition to partaking in this commonplace private act of self-bathing, this high ranking general has to enter Israel's main river, the name of which connotes to "go down."

Up until this point in the story, Naaman has only been described. Now he speaks, and in doing so, grants both readers and those accompanying him a very candid glimpse of his self-perception and political allegiance. With five verbal phrases, he details the drama he thought would unfold. He expected that "he (the prophet) would come out," "that he would stand," "that he would call on the name of Yahweh his God," "that he would wave his hand over the spot," and "that he would cure me" (v. 11). The actual scenario not only fails to conform to the general's plan, but proves insulting. At the very least, he expected an audience with the prophet; Naaman's burst of outrage indicates he actually anticipated much more. Naaman expected that something would be done for him. Instead, he is commanded to go do something for himself. His tirade reveals his expectations, but it also reveals something more. That the prophet failed to appear and do as Naaman expected challenges this high-ranking official's sense of entitlement and self-importance. Naaman's ego itself is on the line. The general's angry oration shows his supposed greatness to be what it really is—merely superficial and self-serving.

His outrage extends beyond the wound that Elisha's instructions and failure to appear inflict on the general's ego. Naaman's rant continues, now navigated by another impediment to receiving a cure: "Are not Abana and Pharpar, rivers of Damascus, better than the water of Israel? Could I not wash in them and be cleansed?" (v. 12). Like the Jordan in Israel, Abana and Pharpar are rivers of national distinction in Aram. Abana waters the oasis wherein the great capital city of Damascus is located. Pharpar, a river south of the capital, irrigates the farmlands upon which Damascus depends. Naaman's shortsighted nationalism manifests itself here. As a proud military general of Aram, his allegiance to all that stands for Syrian supremacy over Israel is clear. Washing in the Jordan constitutes an insult to his steadfast patriotism to Syria. Having first made public his raw egotism, Naaman erects another barrier to his cure. He resorts to parsing the prophet's instructions in nationalistic terms, claiming Damascus's (Syrian) waters as superior to Israel's waters.

The veil on Naaman's greatest challenges to a full recovery falls away. Two gigantic stumbling blocks stand in the way of wholeness—the hurdles of egotism and nationalism. And as he makes clear to those in earshot what is at stake for him, he does so riddled with anger. Two times the narrative relates that Naaman went off in a rage (vv. 11, 12). These two expressions of fury precede and follow his two rhetorical outbursts, where his allegiance to self and allegiance to Aram are revealed.

Naaman went off in a rage . . . (v. 11)

> "I thought he would surely come out and
> stand and
> call on the name of Yahweh, his God and His egotism
> wave his hand over the spot and
> cure me of my a skin disease. (v. 11)
>
> Are not Abana and Pharpar, the rivers of Damascus,
> Better than any of the water of Israel? His nationalism

> Could I not wash in them and be cleansed?"
> And so he went off in a rage. (v. 12)

Naaman's rage surrounds and preserves the faulty logic that threatens to curtail the possibility for a cure. His fury locks him in the twofold argument, trapping him in a prison that separates him from the possibility of wholeness.

Naaman expresses his dismay, presumably to those who have accompanied him on this journey. At this point in the narrative, those in attendance are only implied. They are the invisible others to whom he expresses his outrage and defends his resistance to cooperate with the prophet's plan. Though not yet formally introduced into the narrative, their veiled presence is inferred. Standing by silently, they receive Naaman's angry excuses. He evidently trusts they will agree with him, and he certainly does not worry that they will judge him. With his concluding two-part rhetorical question about the superiority of the rivers in Damascus, Naaman seems to invite their confirmation of his arguments for resisting the prophet's commands. Who are these bystanders, witnessing, but not yet weighing in, on the unfolding events?

"Now the servants of Naaman went to him and said . . ." (v. 13). For the first time, we realize they are his servants. Finally introduced, they emerge as bit-part characters that he has been addressing all this time. As servants, they withhold their opinion and reserve their interpretation of the events. As servants, they have to receive Naaman's expression of frustration across his laborious diatribe of failed and shortsighted expectations. They have to remain silent about what they may perceive as a man ensnared in his own self-importance and false sense of nationalism. Now confronted with Naaman's rhetorical questions, these servants are summoned to corroborate his reasoning for why he should not follow the prophet's directives. However, as servants, they likely resist the nationalism and social milieu that make them servants. They probably have their own view of what makes one important and what makes for real greatness. Thus, called upon by Naaman to confirm his limited vision, they are placed in a bind. They must remain faithful to Naaman, whom they serve, while also remaining faithful to themselves and their perception of actual virtue.

Characteristic of their status playing bit parts, they will speak, but only briefly. Yet it will have a determining effect upon the outcome of Naaman's crisis. Using an endearing term, the servants break through Naaman's angry rage and address him. They call him "My father" (v. 13). In response to Naaman's rhetorical question about the rivers of Damascus, they shift the focus and issue their own rhetorical inquiry: "If the prophet had told you to do something great would you not have done it?" (v. 13). With this carefully crafted response, the servants accomplishment is twofold. First, they avoid having to concur with what they may well perceive as faulty reasoning on the part of their general. Additionally, they redirect Naaman's attention away from his own argumentative gridlock to a place where he can gain some insight. Thus, they actively serve Naaman with their brief speech.

The servants' rhetorical question works to preserve Naaman's limited understanding of what constitutes greatness for now, while allowing him to be receptive to the prophet's offer. In an effort to prevent Naaman from derailing the cure, they play on Naaman's faulty sense of what constitutes his greatness to rupture his egotistical impasse. "If the prophet had told you to do something great would you not have done it? How much more when he bids you, 'wash and be cleansed'?" (v. 13). With shrewd rhetorical strategy, they draw Naaman in and pave the way for his self-reflection. As a military general, Naaman is accustomed to performing great tasks. He leads armies into battle, strategizes major operations and advises the king on international matters of conflict. But the heart of the servants' proposal argues that a small task is much easier to perform than a large undertaking. For Naaman, with his obsession for greatness, the opposite is the case.[32] Thus, the servants invite Naaman to an insight about himself and a new idea about what makes for real greatness. Can Naaman possibly stoop to do only a small thing in order to be healed? Will his greatness be compromised merely by his washing in the Jordan? Can any greatness come from performing small tasks? Or, put in other words, does greatness actually have anything to do with the magnitude of the tasks one performs?

The servants' gentle challenge to their master demonstrates their authentic superiority to one like Naaman. In response to his question, they make their own inquiry of him, tactfully urging the war hero to make his own discovery of what is at stake. In nudging him to an insight and experience beyond his superficial notion of greatness, they necessarily draw upon their own wellspring of insight and experience.

As servants, they are often only involved in behind-the-scenes chores. They perform the menial jobs that go unrecognized or that no one else wants to perform. Often, the work they do allows others to assume center stage or enables others to advance. Yet this is precisely why they are likely in a better position to understand what constitutes genuine greatness or real importance in life. Just as the servant girl did, these servants make way for Naaman to achieve wholeness. While serving as bit-part characters in the story, they play a significant role in the tale. They foster others' well-being, even providing life-giving services for one in need. Perhaps it is precisely this work that puts them in touch with a more enduring sense of what counts.

As we study further the servants in this biblical story, we discover that the poignant contrast between the portrait of Naaman and that of his servants is also instructive. Anger punctuates Naaman's response to his situation and threatens to bar him from the healing that is at hand. By contrast, the servants attempt to defuse his rage by addressing him with the title "My father." With this salutation, they inject calmness into the circumstances at hand and work to reverse the hostile mood. With an excess of words, Naaman tries to convince himself and perhaps those listening why he cannot possibly do that which he deems beneath him. The servants instead practice an economy of speech and resist entering the argumentative fray. They refrain from debating whether Naaman's two-part argument is well grounded. Instead, they speak in a way that makes it possible for the general to move beyond his own impasse.

Throughout the story, much is revealed about Naaman, his life circumstances and even his interiority. The servants, by contrast, remain cloaked in anonymity. We don't know their names or how many they are. No narrative of what service they perform occurs in this account. Their appearance is brief. Still, fixing our attention on these players, this brief encounter between Naaman and his servants reveals a great deal about them. These servants are evidently a compelling and reliable group, as they have been chosen to accompany him on this unusual journey. Naaman's willingness to express his indignation to them suggests his trust in them. But the strongest argument for how compelling this group is resides in Naaman's response to the only speech they make. Immediately after they gently lay bare the real choice before the general, Naaman acts on their encouragement. In contrast to Naaman's self-serving egotism, the servants understand what is at stake. In contrast to Naaman's sense of entitlement, this group of individuals seems only to act out of fidelity and service to another. Once their service is rendered, and true to their status as bit-part characters, they disappear from the story—the story that has been redirected precisely because of their intervention.

CONCLUSION

In the act that follows, often referred to as Naaman's Conversion (vv. 15–19), the general stands before the prophet and professes his faith. The servant girl and Naaman's servants disappear from the story. But characteristic of these members of the supporting cast, resonances of their impact on behalf of Naaman continue to echo. The text reads, "Naaman went back with his attendants to the man of God and stood *before* him (Elisha)" (v. 15). The prescription for a cure, as proposed by the little servant girl, is now fulfilled. The detours designed by Naaman and his king that would have preserved his false sense of greatness have been completely redirected: "Naaman stands before the prophet." Moreover, the phrase "stands before" communicates even more explicitly the sense of service and allegiance than the language of the servant girl's proposal, "was before the prophet."[33] Hence, the servant girl's original plan for Naaman is not only fulfilled, but actually surpassed, when he "stands before the prophet." As he professes his faith and service to the prophet concerning Israel's God, his cure apparently extends beyond mere physical wellness. The servant girl risked exercising her faith in God's healing power for this foreign general. When belief is so bold on the part of one so seemingly insignificant, the divine intervention appears to exceed what the agent herself could even have imagined. Naaman's skin disease is cured, but he also now professes a faith in her God.

The impact of Naaman's servants also persists in this second scene, though they have been excused from the narrative. Were it not for the wisdom of his own servants, who coaxed him to self-reflection, Naaman might have returned home infirmed, humiliated, and still in a rage. When he finally stands before the prophet and confesses his faith in God, Naaman refers to himself as "servant." Thus, Naaman, the great military general, refers to himself five times (vv. 15, 17a, 17b, 18a, 18b) with the term "your servant," the very term used to designate those who fostered his healing at the Jordan.[34] Like his servants, who minister to him, Naaman now calls himself a servant before the prophet and before the Lord. But Naaman's servants surpass Naaman in this role. Naaman stands only in humble abeyance before the prophet and his Lord. Naaman's servants stood in an advisory role before their master. Hence, the action of his servants, which eventually transforms Naaman's flesh to be like that of "a little child," also pushes him to acknowledge his status as "servant" as he confesses his faith.

The great chasm separating the so-called "major" character, Naaman, and the nameless members of the supporting cast, the servant girl and Naaman's servants, begins to collapse. In faith and as servants, a kinship unfolds between Naaman and his servants and Naaman and the servant girl. That which seemed to separate characters in the narrative scheme reveals itself to be unfounded. Moreover, what appears to separate servants and masters might also be faulty, both in this story and in reality. Heroism often reveals itself to be an artificial cultural designation that, when abandoned, exposes others who truly qualify for such ranks.

The service rendered by the servant girl and Naaman's servants, both in the progression of the narrative and in Naaman's quest for a cure, becomes an important instruction offered by this tale. Thus, as we conclude this study of these servant characters, we may even decide that of all the courage, wisdom, and personal strength expended in this story, theirs have perhaps been the greatest.

Such a discovery emancipates the reader from the injustices of the narrative caste system (major versus minor characters). It encourages us to engender alternative reading practices that might result in a more equitable and just assessment of all the characters present. This, in turn, can cultivate a new sensitivity toward our own context. Perhaps it might even engender a more equitable and justice-based assessment of those residing among us. Bit part members of the supporting cast bear significance and worth, despite their quiet presence and reduced visibility. Such an awareness challenges us to recognize the impoverishment that results if we resist acknowledging the virtue and contributions of their counterparts in our own world.

NOTES

1. https://dictionary.cambridge.org/us/dictionary/english/bit-part.

2. In theater, bit part characters are confined to reciting no more than five lines of dialogue. See https://backstage.zendesk.com/hc/en-us/articles/115005472843-A-Glossary-of-Acting-Terms.

3. An earlier version of this study appeared in *Scripture and Social Justice: Catholic Ecumenical Essays,* eds. Anathea A. Portier-Young and Gregory A. Sterling (Lanham, MD: Lexington Books/Fortress Press, 2017), 107–24.

4. While the NRSV translates the Hebrew here as "leprosy" its biblical representations in the bible, especially in Leviticus 13–14 do not coincide with the clinical depiction of leprosy (known as Hansesn's disease) See Steven McKenzie, *1 Kings-2Kings 16 IECOT Commentary* (Stuttgart, Germany: W. Kohlmanner, 2019), 301.

5. Terence Fretheim, *First and Second Kings* (Louisville, KY: Westminster John Knox Press, 1999), 154–55; Paul R. House, *1, 2 Kings—The New American Commentary* (Nashville: Broadman & Holman Publishers, 1995), 274; and Robert L. Cohn, *2 Kings Berit Olam: Studies in Hebrew Narrative and Poetry* (Collegeville, MN: The Liturgical Press, 2000), 42.

6. See Mordechai Cogan and Hayim Tadmor, *The Anchor Bible, II Kings* (Garden City, NJ: Doubleday, 1988), 61–67, and Jean Kyoung Kim, "Reading and Retelling Naaman's Story (2 Kings 5)," *Journal for the Study of the Old Testament* 30 (2005): 49–61.

7. ¹Richard Nelson, *First and Second Kings: Interpretation* (Knoxville, TN: John Knox Press, 1987), 183.

8. See Nancy Haught, *Sacred Strangers: What the Bible's Outsiders Can Teach Christians* (Collegeville, MN: Liturgical Press, 2017), 47–58, a study that celebrates the great faith of this foreign general for all its radicality and what an outsider like Naaman can teach about humility and gratitude.

9. T. R. Hobbs, *2 Kings Word Book Commentary* (Waco, TX: Word Publishers, 1985), 58–62.

10. Adele Berlin, *Poetics and Interpretation of Biblical Narrative* (Winona Lake, IN: Eisenbrauns, 1994), defines the character group "agents" as those characters who achieve significance only in so far as they perform a function for the narrative or in the service of the plot, 31–32. Such an identification and definition of a character works to bracket the sense of person implied, thereby rendering them unimportant for themselves.

11. Alex Woloch, *The One vs. the Many: Minor Characters and the Space of the Protagonist in the Novel* (Princeton, NJ: Princeton University Press, 2003), who notes that "For Marx, utilitarianism's theft of experience . . . results from the actual expropriation of the labor-power of the many by the few. As utilization covers over the exploitation that inheres in the social structure, so character-function effaces the narrative subordination that produces minor characters," 28–29.

12. Gerhard von Rad hinted at her importance as well as the other servants when he observed that the great one will be helped by the lowly ones in the story in "Naaman: A Critical Retelling," in *God at Work in Israel,* trans. J. H. Mark. (Nashville: Abingdon Press, 1980), 48.

13. This antithesis has been frequently noted in previous studies. See Robert Cohn, "Form and Perspective in 2 Kings V" *VT* 31 (1983): 174; Rick Dale Moore, *God Saves: Lessons from the Elisha Stories* (Sheffield, UK: Sheffield Academic Press, 1990), 71–72; Burke Long, *2 Kings: Forms of the Old Testament Literature,* vol X. (Grand Rapids, MI: William B. Eerdmans Publishing Company, 1991), 70.

14. For a discussion of skin diseases and the related social and religious stigmas of translating Naaman's condition as "leprosy" see S. G. Browne, *Leprosy in the Bible* (2nd ed.; London:

Christina Medical Fellowship, 1986), and "Leprosy in the bible," in *Medicine & the Bible* ed. B. Palmer (Carlisle, U.K: Paternoster, 1986), 101–27.

15. Biblical quotes follow the author's translation.

16. Her status, though not designated with the Hebrew word for "servant," is indisputable. As a foreign prisoner, she is before (לִפְנֵי) the wife of Naaman in his house. See discussion to follow (10-11) on לִפְנֵי (*lipně*) as paying allegiance or service to a superior.

17. Hobbs, 63; John Gray, *I & II Kings: A Commentary* (Philadelphia: Westminster Press, 1970), 504.

18. Contra Esther M. Menn, "A Little Child Shall Lead Them: The Role of the Little Israelite Servant Girl (2 Kings 5. 1-19)," *Currents in Theology and Mission* 35 (October 2008), who interprets "if only" as "the girl's words expressing a wish contrary to fact," 343.

19. See *A Hebrew and English Lexicon of the Old Testament,* eds. Francis Brown, S. R. Driver, and C. A. Briggs (Oxford, UK: Clarendon, 1907), 816.

20. Samson agrees to pay anyone who can solve his riddle during the seven-day feast with thirty linen garments and thirty sets of clothing (Judges 14:12). Joseph, in his capacity as viceroy in Egypt, presents each of his brothers with a set of clothing and gives Benjamin four sets of clothing (Genesis 45:22).

21. Leviticus 13:44–46 prescribes exile from the community for them. Even governing officials were not exempt from these social consequences. When leprosy broke out on the forehead of Judah's King Uzziah, he was hurried from the temple where he was officiating and no longer allowed to serve as king (2 Chron 26:16–21).

22. Robert Wilson, *Prophecy and Society in Ancient Israel* (Philadelphia: Fortress Press, 1980), 42ff., and Thomas Overholt, *Channels of Prophecy: The Social Dynamics of Prophetic Activity* (Minneapolis, MN: Fortress Press, 1989), 3ff.

23. On central vs. peripheral prophets, see Wilson, 38–40.

24. Toward the end of his career in the traditions, however, Elisha does facilitate the overthrow of the Omride dynasty and the initiation of Jehu's reign in Israel.

25. Tamaris Renteria Hoover, "The Elijah/Elisha Stories: A Sociocultural Analysis of Prophets and People in Ninth-Century B.C.E. Israel," *Elisha and Elisha in Socioliterary Perspective,* ed. Robert Coote (Atlanta, GA: Scholars Press, 1992) argues this thesis.

26. On two other occasions, King Jehoram responds consistent with the same despairing demeanor portrayed here. In 2 Kings 6:31, he blames the prophet and God for the starvation of the citizens of Samaria. and in 2 Kings 3:10, this ruler blames God for what he perceives as the defeat of Israel before Moab.

27. Typically, the theme of inclusivity is grounded in Naaman, the foreign general who comes to faith in God after being cured of his leprosy, in contrast to Gehazi, the Israelite who acts contrary to faith and ends up with leprosy. See Hobbs, 66, and Moore, 83–84.

28. Typically, the theme of inclusivity is grounded in Naaman, the foreign general who comes to faith in God after being cured of his leprosy, in contrast to Gehazi, the Israelite who acts contrary to faith and ends up with leprosy. See Hobbs, 66, and Moore, 83–84.

29. Walter Bruggemann, *1 & 2 Kings: Smyth & Helwys Bible Commentary* (Macon, GA: Smyth & Helwys Publishing Incorporated, 2000), 234; Fretheim, 153; and Cohn, *2 Kings*, 38.

30. Noticed also by Terence Fretheim, *Deuteronomistic History* (Nashville: Abingdon Press, 1983), 150; Robert L. Cohn, "Form and Perspective," 177; and Moore, 73.

31. Henry O. Thompson, "Jordan River," *Anchor Bible Dictionary*, vol. 3, ed. David Noel Freedman (New York: Doubleday, 1992), 954.

32. Moore, 76.

33. Ibid., 78.

34. Ibid., 78. Also noted by Fretheim, 153; and Hermann Gunkel, *Elias, Jahve und Baal.* Religionsgeschichtliche Volksbucher, 2/2 (Tubingen, Germany: Mohr, 1906), 39.

Chapter Five

Vessels of Hope versus Hallmarks of Despair

A Study of Cameo Appearance Characters in 2 Kings 4:1–7

How often we pass by people who appear only once in our lives' journeys! And if we were to define these various individuals by this passing encounter on the street, for example, we likely would label them according to the "types" by which we organize our perception of that particular social context. "Types" is one of the categories with which the Bible's so-called minor characters have been labeled in the past.[1] They were viewed as representing a category of persons whom readers could quickly classify. They were "mothers," "merchants," "cultic officials," "warriors," "servants," "court officials," and so on. Such labels granted them the most abbreviated definition as characters, and thus they assumed their silent role as part of the societal context of the story. Identified by only one word, typically denied any speech, and characteristically made to appear and disappear in the least noteworthy of fashion, their value as persons, or even their status as characters, was never pursued. Yet these are the individuals in the story that mirror the thousands of individuals we pass by in our lives. And while this momentary notice leaves them shrouded in anonymity, we also acknowledge that pausing to chat with any one of them would grant us a closer, more appreciative understanding of who they are. We might even ascribe to them some value as persons if we encounter them again.

It is no secret that a stroll on a downtown street in Manhattan urges us to label many folks by their appearance or by the way they move down the street. They are to us "business men," "street people," "a hospital worker," "a restaurant server," "a construction foreman," and so on, all by virtue of their appearance and how they travel past us. But such labels not only may be incorrect; they also limit the description of who these individuals are and the story that defines them.

Characters in a story that occur only once and have nothing to say are not unlike the people we pass on the street. But unlike those encounter, these characters typically lack any description. We don't see what they are wearing. We miss hearing them talking on their cell phones or mumbling to themselves or uttering some expletive at someone who bumps into them. We don't see their facial expressions. We can't capture how briskly or wearily they move. All the cues we enlist to craft initial impressions about those for whom we lack information are absent when we pass by their counterparts in the narrative world. In a story, we typically are afforded only one word describing the cameo appearance characters before they disappear. They never have a name and frequently appear in groups. Mentioned only by the narrator in crafting the conditions or circumstances of the story, these supporting cast characters hardly command our attention. They are "the crowd," "the slaves," "the servant girl," "the reapers." If they are given any mention at all in interpretive commentaries, they are viewed as serving the narrative infrastructure. At best, they are credited with crafting the scenery, establishing the nature of the social world, or contributing to the notoriety of the main characters. For example, the mention of "the servants" or "the slaves" helps to sketch a milieu with a presumed social stratification. Or a passing reference to "the quarrymen" or "the builders" colors the scenery of a narrative with the construction projects of those with power, such as kings, who could command such endeavors. Or the wealth of the protagonist landowner might be best illustrated with the passing mention of his "foremen," "laborers," or "harvesters."

Such brief and delimited appearances render this third group of the supporting cast as the cameo appearance members. Some might resist assigning them such a designation. Indeed, the term "cameo appearance" typically spotlights persons of some renown or notoriety who, though making only very brief appearances in plays or films, are recognized by the public. But this is precisely why these almost invisible characters, whom we tend to read past, are grouped here as "cameo appearances." Such a label works in the service of the project's larger objective. In an effort to redefine this easily passed over, anonymous group of the supporting cast, the designation "cameo appearances" signals that they, too, are of some renown when consideration is granted to them. They, too, are worthy of notice. Even though they make the briefest of appearances, they summon recognition by readers. So, the label "cameo appearance group" implies that even the characters who appear only momentarily on the set also deserve recognition and, thus, are worth studying.

Admittedly, their incredibly thin description makes them a challenge to investigate. They emerge in the narrative by a single identifier that usually occurs only once—"townspeople," "merchants," "maiden," "foreigners," and so on. We pass by them in our reading as we do people on the sidewalk. And while those passed by in real life have visual, audible, olfactory, and physical cues to help inform our limited perceptions of them, those we read in the story world seem, at first glance, to have little that can be said about their person. However, a prolonged encounter with any character from the cameo appearance group might reveal that they are not as svelte, stultified, and one-dimensional as we might be tempted, at first glance, to conclude. While the initial encounter of a passing mention of "the servant" or "the spinners" might suggest a lack of any substantive basis for analysis, marshalling our potential as readers might disclose something more. In contrast to people we pass by on the sidewalk, the encounter with the one-time appearance of a character in a story is a place where readers can choose to dwell. We can stop and ask questions. We can interrogate the story world and the surrounding narrative about this individual. If we choose, readers can investigate the role such characters play in excess of their limited appearance in the story. A search for relevant sociohistorical background information can thicken and color the initial, shadowy silhouettes of the individuals suggested by cameo appearances. Their counterparts in other stories, who are more extensively drawn, also can be enlisted to help elaborate their personas and suggest their implied stories. Moreover, some cameo appearance characters actually play a central role in the story in which they appear. However, because their presence is so brief and their description so limited, the essential nature of their contribution is easily missed, passed over, or even taken for granted. But a prolonged study of these often by-passed individuals has the potential to reveal much more.

AN EXAMPLE: 2 KINGS 4:1–7

Second Kings 4:1–7 registers as the first of four stories featuring five miracles illustrating the power of Elisha, the prophet across this chapter. In the previous chapter, Elisha displayed his miraculous activities in a very public and national sphere, assisting the armies of Israel, Edom, and Judah in their military conflict against Moab. By contrast, in this chapter, he acts in more domestic and local settings that include the households of an unnamed widow (vv. 1–7) and the Shunnamite woman (vv. 8–37), a meal with the brotherhood of prophets (vv. 38–41), and the famine of a village (vv. 42–44). Moreover, the four stories across this chapter are not only united by the persistent intervention of Elisha; they all manifest the thematic shift of life rescued from death. Despite its brevity and simplicity, this first story (vv. 1–7) introduces and illustrates this dramatic movement from the threat of death to the promise of life that governs all these accounts.

This uncomplicated tale (2 Kgs 4:1–7) begins with an encounter between a woman and Elisha. the prophet. While most commentaries and Bibles label this brief story with a focus upon Elisha, that is, "Elisha and the Miraculous Jug of Oil" or "Elisha Helps a Poor Widow," the woman is the first to speak in the narrative. The wife of one of the followers of Elisha, she has lost her husband. The widow addresses the prophet and, without explicitly asking for his help, sets before him the crisis she now faces. Her husband left her a widow with dependents. Now a creditor is threatening to take her two children as slaves if she does not settle some outstanding debts (v. 1).[2] Initially, the prophet asks her what he can do about this. Then he asks what she has in her house. At first, the widow reports that she has nothing of value in her house. And then, almost as an afterthought, she adds that she does have one thing. She still has "one pouring of oil" (v. 2).[3] The prophet instructs her to gather jars from all her neighbors and, with her two children, shut the door of her house and start pouring her oil into all the jars that she and her children have gathered (vv. 3–4). She does as the prophet instructs. Next, we hear that she shuts the door behind herself and her children, and she starts pouring the oil (v. 5). She fills all the jars with oil until one of her children announces that there are no more jars (v. 6). Finally, she goes back to the prophet and reports what has occurred. In turn, he tells her to sell the oil, pay off her debts. As a final note, he adds that she and her children can live on the surplus that is left (v. 7).

The structure of the story mirrors the simplicity of the narrative itself. An encounter between the woman and the prophet at both the beginning and end of the story (vv. 1–4, 7) encloses a narrative featuring the actions by the widow and the miraculous unfolding in her house (vv. 5–6). Despite its brevity, this simple tale hosts not only several members of the cameo appearance group, but an array of supporting cast characters, all of whom play essential and important roles. The widow and her dialogue with the prophet, along with the narrative focus upon her actions, cast her in a key *complementary role* as a supporting cast member. She has real staying power in the story. She not only initiates the dialogue with the prophet at the opening of the story, but also initiates their second, and final, encounter, which closes the tale. Further, because she takes the lead in approaching the prophet and she exhibits a clear willingness to carry out his instructions, she has a good deal of influence determining the outcome of the plot. Thus, she wields a significant hand in the unfolding of this account. Moreover, she is even conscripted with a good deal of direct discourse, despite the very abbreviated nature of this story. The plot turns on the woman's obedience to the prophet's instructions. Her willingness to approach the prophet and, subsequently, follow his directives implies a faith in Yahweh, the God for whom the prophet is an agent. Finally, the crisis of the story resolves, in part, because the actions of the widowed woman bring about her own change of destiny.

Her two children are briefly referenced in the opening encounter between their mother and the prophet. They also number among the supporting cast. Together, they play *bit parts*. That they are the children, whom a creditor has threatened to take as slaves from their mother, provides the brief, but requisite, description about them. Their fate is not only desperate but central to the multilayered nature and depth of the crisis. Moreover, the threat to their well-being also intensifies the gravity of their widowed mother's fate. The story reveals that, not only has the woman lost her husband, but the children have suffered the loss of a father. They now must depend upon a widowed woman in a man's world. They are residents in a society whose laws do not protect them. Instead, they become commodities by means of which debts are settled. In the process, they not only endure the loss of a father, but they might also be stripped of the little security to which they could cling. They are about to be taken from their mother and made slaves.

When the prophet issues directives to the woman, he includes the children in the instructions. He directs that she and her children gather vessels and shut the door of their house behind them. Later, the narrative reveals more about the children. One is identified as a son (v. 6) and the two of them are to assist their mother gathering jars and passing them to her as she pours oil. In addition, as the miracle unfolds, the son has a brief speaking role. When his mother requests that they pass another jug to her, it falls to him to announce that "there are no more" (v. 6). The recognition and announcement that the miracle is complete falls from the lips of one of these two children. He gives witness to the conclusion of their effort, which will reverse both he and his sibling's fate, as well as restore both the widow and her children to life. At the end of this short account, the two youngsters are referenced again. The prophet instructs the widow that she is to sell the oil, pay off the debts, and then she and her two children can live on the rest. Not only the widow, but her two young children, has become the recipients of a renewed future. Restored to the assurance of safety and security of their mother's care, the conclusion bears witness to the scope of the miracle's effect. Though playing only *bit parts,* the children reside at the heart of the crisis, which eventually yields to a life-giving resolution.

But the mother and the children are not the only supporting cast members in this story. In addition to these characters playing *complementary roles* and *bit parts*, another set of supporting cast members reside in this account. In the very first verse of our story, two members of the cameo appearance group are introduced. The brotherhood of prophets is referenced in conjunction with the widow's plea to Elisha. Her late husband had belonged to that community. And, in that same opening overture to the prophet, her plea for assistance rests on the God-fearing disposition of the second member of this group, her now-deceased husband. She reminds Elisha of her husband's God-fearing fidelity as an incentive to gain the prophet's assistance. In addition, two additional members of the *cameo appearance* group also figure significantly in the narrative. In this chapter, these two characters will be the focus of this exposition.

THE CREDITOR

The first of these other two cameo appearance characters, "a creditor" registers in the woman's opening plea to Elisha. Mentioned only once (v. 1), the creditor constitutes the central threat, instigating her predicament and prompting her pursuit of the prophet for assistance. The report of a creditor gives reason for this story. Were there no creditor, there would be no crisis. Hence, because the story stems from this sole mention of a creditor and of his claim on her children, his character, easy to read past, rises in significance.

Some villainize creditors, suggesting they contribute to the build-up of social and economic inequities.[4] Those in debt must borrow money and, in the process, finance the wealth of creditors. When creditors appear in the same realm as the economically threatened, such as a widow, they often merit a particularly unpopular reputation. If a creditor is part of the Israelite community, their economic superiority might be qualified by the laws of release (Deut 15:1–18) and Jubilee (Lev 25), which ultimately required the excusing of obliged individuals from debt. Whether the practice was actually carried out is difficult to determine.[5]

At first glance, there is no direct indication that the creditor is part of the larger Israelite community or is constrained by such legal obligations. Anonymous, and identified merely as "a creditor," he makes only one appearance in the woman's narrative about him. However, the woman's request is not a request for protection under the law. The creditor's plan, in the instance of unpaid debt, actually coincides with Israelite law. According to these legal traditions, if a person's debt is unpaid, the creditor may seize the property or children of the debtor (Exod 21:7; Isa 50:1; Amos 2:6, 8:6; Mic 2:9; Neh 5:3–5). The existence of such laws, and the reference to these transactions by the prophets, serve as an initial indication of the creditor's probable affiliation within the larger community of Israel. That the prophet's scheme does not protect the woman from the creditor's demand, but rather seeks to address the monetary obligation, suggests further that the creditor can be presumed to be an Israelite acting well within his legal rights.

While it is clear that the creditor intends to collect on the outstanding debt, its origin is uncertain. The unpaid financial commitment may have originated from the widow's husband, who may have died before he could repay his obligation. However, because conditions of poverty often necessitated loans, the debt may have stemmed from the family's deteriorating economic situation due to the husband's death.

On face value, the biblical tradition indicates that the necessity for loans and those who made them was a well-recognized practice in monarchic Israel. Laws existed to regulate these negotiations and to limit creditors from requiring interest from those with pay back obligations. Forgoing the profit that came from interest was grounded in the care of the community that God had brought out of Egypt, liberating them from slavery.[6] When one member of the community was in need, a loan without interest was the care to be given in the name of the LORD, "who brought you out of the land of Egypt (Lev 25:35–38). Such legal texts suggest that some people did not possess adequate economic means at different times of their lives and thus required financial assistance. Creditors with good financial know-how, and not driven solely by profit, could benefit the community. Thus, the identification of an individual as a creditor does not, by necessity, warrant condemnation. Nor does it necessarily suggest a malicious individual.

However, a sociohistorical investigation of the creditor in this story may reveal otherwise. Who is this creditor? The Masoretic text situates the Elijah and Elisha narratives, which include this story, within the monarchic era of the Omrides. This first real dynasty in Israel (Omri, Ahab, Ahaziah, and Jehoram) was known for its development of extensive trade routes and building projects. Some scholars have proposed that the Omride building projects "put extreme economic pressure on the citizens of Israel."[7] The status of small, free landowners probably deteriorated in the face of creditors, and a drought that occurred during Ahab's kingship may have forced many of them to go into debt or even lose their land.[8] Ahab, the successor to his father's Omri kingship, so heavily burdened the peasants working on the land in order to accomplish these projects that he is often referred to as the Solomon of the North.[9] Taxation, the monopoly of resources and services among the state and private elite, and high interest loans financed these projects while, at the same time, led to the collapse of control by local kinship groups. Peasants would be forced to seek frequent survival loans from creditors privileged with economic means or surplus. The rise of debt slavery can be attributed to the insolvency among free citizens caused by these shifts in both economic factors and social stratification tied to this monarchy. Moreover, debt instruments, such as confiscating children as slaves in repayment of loans, became the means of a second and escalating round of surplus extraction by creditors.[10] As evidenced in the prophetic writings of the ninth and eighth centuries, the relationship between Israel's elite and peasant citizens on the land was one of exploitation. The prophets in Israel made it clear that during this period the peasantry and small farmers were particularly vulnerable to wealthy private and state elite and landowners, who readily took them in as debt slaves (1 Kgs 21; Amos 2:6–8, 5:8–12; Hosea 4:2, 5:10, 12:7–8

[Heb 8–9]). That these sociopolitical circumstances form the backdrop of this tale begins to tarnish the character of the creditor who has come to take the widow's children as slaves.

Specifically, it is the circumstances of the woman as a widow and the creditor's intention to enslave her children that raise questions about his character. The woman is a widow, one of the three subjects, along with the orphan and the foreigner, the care of whom the community of Israel was repeatedly summoned (Exod 22:21–24; Deut 27:19; 10:18; 14:28–29; 24:17, 19) Often the instruction to extend this care is accompanied by the motive for laying this obligation upon members of the community: "Remember you were once a slave in Egypt and that is why I am commanding you to do this" (Exod 22:21–24; Deut 24:22).

Though he is well within the law, there is hardheartedness about this creditor's plan to enact his legal prerogative and take possession of her children. Though widowed in this patriarchal society, and thus more subject to poverty, the widow does have two children (v. 1), one of whom is identified as a son (v. 6). And while the description of them indicates that they are still young children (*yeledim*) and thus dependent upon her, the prospect of two children, one of whom is a son, gives definition and potential prosperity for this widow's future. Obliged now to care for them, in the future they may well be the means of care for her. A woman in a patriarchal society has place and identity by virtue of the men with whom she is affiliated, whether he be a father, a husband, a son, or a male relative. Her poverty (she claims that she has nothing in her house except one pouring of oil) suggests that any connection with a male extended male family member, if he even exists, affords no security. Moreover, that she has to be solely responsible for outstanding debts also indicates her solitary status economically in the community. The existence of children with at least one of them being a son, and the potential that children promise, may well be her only hope. Deprived of both husband and sons, and with nothing in her house, she has no prospects.

The toll that such a comprehensive loss takes on an Israelite woman is well documented in the Book of Ruth. Naomi, considers herself destitute, not merely because of her husband's death, but because of the subsequent death of her two sons Malhon and Chilon (Ruth 1:1–8). Even in the face of her daughter-in-law Ruth's unfathomable pledge of solidarity (1:16–17), Naomi considers herself indigent and claims a new name for herself, "Mara" (meaning "bitter"), when she returns to her own land, Bethlehem (1:20). Without the security of a husband or sons, she is a lone, widowed woman in a man's world. Similarly, the threatened loss of this widowed woman's two children to a creditor as slaves leaves this woman in similar desperate straits. But beyond what they might provide for her well-being in the future, that they are her young children makes such forfeiture especially egregious for a mother.

Such an enactment by this creditor does seem merciless; whether the creditor actually is within his rights to do this must be questioned. The world of the legal texts regarding debt slavery are male-directed and male-dominated. The legal traditions regarding the confiscation of children in the case of unpaid debts are set out in the second person plural to the men of the community. The biblical tradition does allow for the selling of a man's children into slavery in payment of debts. However, it does specify that this obligation is upon the man, father of these children. In the instance of our story, the father of these children no longer exists. Instead, they are now subject to the diminished economic conditions that characterize their widowed mother. No female, rich or poor, is saddled with the obligations of debt repayment or debt slavery. When widows are mentioned in the Covenant Code (Exod 22:21) and in Deuteronomy (24:17, 19), the mandate is one of care for these, the most vulnerable ones, who were without a protective male.[11] In light of what must have been considered such devastating circumstances, Exod 22:22 sets forth mandates against doing harm to or otherwise afflicting the widow and the orphan. The punishment detailed for such abuse is harsh and comprehensive, suggesting the seriousness with which protection of these most vulnerable was urged, as well as abuses that must have existed to warrant such legislation. In addition, Exod 22:24–26 warns against dealing as a creditor with people, particularly the poor of the community to whom one has lent money. Specifically, this intends not exacting interest from those who are already in debt. But the mandate here is directed to Israelite males, who have occasion to lend money to other Israelite males.

While this cameo appearance of "a creditor" might urge reading past this character, his role is very significant and even central to the story. In what, at first glance, appears as a simple tale about a local private matter, the study of "a creditor" in the presumed context of the Omride dynasty discloses much more. The sociopolitical consequences of the Omride dynasty or any hierarchical form of government and its accomplishments are not confined to the level of the state but trickle down and are made pitifully tangible by this creditor's presence in a woman's domestic sphere. What the text does not narrate is also revealing. There is no room for negotiation or leniency in a socially stratified world of the haves and the have-nots. This creditor's loyalties are aligned with the state, and his pockets are likely lined with the growing wealth of the state's elite to which he belongs. The care of the orphan and widow, or even the basic human sentiment that later becomes formal legislation to refrain from harming them, seems not to bind this individual. The profit yielded from acquiring two children as slaves defines and governs his fidelities. Defaulted loans and the subsequent loss of land or even children are the capital that contributes to the build-up of his class. The wealth of the elite, who are identified with the state, stems from the increasing impoverishment of the larger peasant population. That a widowed woman will be deprived of her children, incur incalculable maternal anguish because of such loss, as well as be deprived of the future that a son could offer her seems inconsequential to the creditor when compared to his larger economic gain. A prolonged focus upon the creditor, in conjunction with the sociopolitical milieu in which this story resides, occasions a close-up glance of these transactions and the devastation visited upon those who are powerless to resist them.

At the level of the story world, the cameo appearance of the creditor has created the crisis warranting resolution. Commentaries have suggested a variety of agents essential to the rescue of this widow and her children. Some point out how the "prophetic word" becomes the source of rescue here and elsewhere in the Elisha tradition.[12] Some interpretations note how the prophets themselves use their agency to reverse the fate of the destitute.[13] Still others interpret how the initiative of the widow and her insistence before the prophet became a means to her own salvation.[14] But if we train our reading practice to be more inclusive, we further discover who also should be numbered among the agents of change and restoration in this tale.

THE NEIGHBORS

A second member of the supporting cast, making only a cameo appearance, now emerges and acts in such a way to oppose the threat of the powerful creditor. As part of the prophet's instructions to the woman (v. 3), "the neighbors" are mentioned only once in passing; they have no speaking part and remain anonymous. The prophet commands her to go "gather jars from all your neighbors, and not only a few" (v. 3), and then she is to shut the door behind herself and her children and start pouring. Who are "the neighbors" in Israelite society that the woman is supposed to approach? Neighbors are members of the community. The original meaning of neighbor was "associate." Its frequent occurrence across the Covenant Code indicates that these laws were intended to legislate on behalf of the members of the Israelite community (Exod 20:16–17; Exodus 21:14; Exodus 21:18; Exodus 21:35; Exodus 22:7–11; Exodus 22:14; Exodus 22:26; Exodus 32:27; Exodus 33:11). In Leviticus 19:18, the term clearly referred to a fellow Hebrew. "Do not take revenge or bear a grudge against members of your community, but love your neighbor as yourself; I am Yahweh." Here members of the community are synonymous with neighbors. Moreover, how one treated his or her neighbor determined one's righteousness. In fact, the ill treatment of one's neighbor was both a sign and cause of a community or nation's disintegration (Isa 3:5; Jer 9:4–9; Mic 7:5–6).

Across the Old Testament, the word *neighbor* is most frequently used to describe fellow Israelites, in particular. The notion of neighbor as fellow

Israelites or associates coincided well with the communal framework that characterized pre-monarchic Israel's self-governance in local kinship groups. While the motive for the northern tribes' rejection of monarchy remains uncertain, perhaps a desire to return to a pre-monarchic self-understanding, free from the obligations and oppressions of kingship, instigated its break away after Solomon's death. The later mandate "to love your neighbor as yourself" in Deuteronomy seemed to formalize and underscore the consideration and care for another that was to characterize this community and even override what the law required.

The prophet's instructions to the woman regarding the request to the neighbors is notably specific. The woman is to gather jars from "all your neighbors." That the instructions specify "all (*kol*) your neighbors" indicates not only a sizable number of neighbors, but that all of them are needed for the success of this plan. The instruction implies an encounter of the widow and all her neighbors, in which she will have to ask them for something they can give her. Moreover, implied here is the fact that neighbors will have a decision to make: whether to say "yes" or "no." The woman has no choice. So much is at stake. This may be her only chance to find a solution that may rescue her and her two children from the consequences of the law regarding outstanding debts. By contrast, the neighbors, if they cooperate, do so freely. They have nothing to gain if they do and nothing to lose if they don't.

The prophet's instruction to the widow also insists upon the secrecy of what is to take place.[15] Upon gathering jars, she and her children are to go into her house and shut the door behind them. The drama of what unfolds bars the neighbors from witnessing what she does with the jars. Evidently, the neighbors have to trust for what purpose she needs so many of these containers. Shrouded in secrecy, what occurs behind closed doors excludes the neighbors, who have lent the woman what she needed.

Despite the nature of her request for jars and the secrecy surrounding their purpose, there must have been a clear certainty that the neighbors would provide. The narrative simply skips over that complicated task of the widow and children going from house to house of the neighbors and gathering jugs. Instead, we hear that the family shut the door behind themselves, and as the children handed their mother the jars, she kept pouring. The Hebrew here makes use of participle forms to demonstrate the continuous actions, not only suggesting their participation but also the very large number of jars continuing to be filled. And how many jars did she fill? Well, we don't have a number; but the oil filled enough jars for her to pay off her debts and more. The surplus was enough to support her children and herself. That allows us to imagine a great number of jars, supplied by neighbors, to hold a great amount of oil.

The neighbors and their cooperation were essential to the fulfillment of the prophet's instruction. The neighbors and their generosity were the means to the social change that took place in the life of that widow and her two children. The transition from the threat of loss of her children, her own marginalization, and a further level of economic impoverishment are all reversed by what the story skips over but implies: the neighbors were willing to give. That they agreed to her request for jugs became the means to the renewal of life that took place, not only because of the prophet's word and the woman's initiative; this transition to life and a future also rested upon the participation of this anonymous group, who have no voice and are mentioned only once in the story. We hardly see them. The narrator acknowledges them only once as a nameless collective group. They are given no details or social definition other than the one-time reference as "the neighbors."

Indeed, the neighbors were the agents of change and restoration through their unacknowledged, but implied, cooperation and generosity. They provided the resources of which she had none. Their generosity made it possible for the woman to have jugs to fill. Their jugs became vessels of hope when she was surrounded by hallmarks of despair. The neighbors became grassroots agents of social transformation and empowerment by handing over what they had so that the miracle could unfold. We don't know what it cost them. We don't know if they had to go without as the result of what they gave. We don't know who they were. That they said yes is not even narrated. Their cameo appearance is only a slight thread in this larger narrative in which their role and importance easily may be missed. Still, the story's successful outcome hinges upon their generosity. It bears evidence of their virtue, their unacknowledged giving, and their willingness to be community for this widow and her children. Well-known author and feminist bell hooks, talks about community as "keepers of hope."[16] And hope becomes a means of empowerment for those for whom all else seems hopeless.

But the neighbors are more than community for the widow. They become formatters of their own ongoing character. Virtue, when practiced on behalf of another, not only forms an individual's character but also becomes a means to the formation of who a community becomes when practiced by the community.[17] It fashions "not simply the particular, historical and diverse communities but, more importantly, moral communities for moral characters are an inherent and constitutive element of a community."[18] Hence, such behavior, when practiced by a communal group such as "all the neighbors," generates and sustains not just a member, like the widow, but the community, by shaping its identity and its moral formation.

CONCLUSION

The creditor and the neighbors form two opposing poles of the story. One constitutes a threat and the other offers a promise. Their occurrence in the same story may also reveal the tension between two competing societal configurations. The creditor and his role in the story represent the increasing build-up of a socially stratified society, in which the few wealthy, powerful individuals at the top control, and even take advantage of, the ever-increasing and impoverished population at the bottom. The neighbors narrate an alternative society of a more egalitarian, self-governing kinship group of earlier days before the monarchy. Though supported by Israelite law, the creditor gives no evidence of any human concern that would be moved by the dire straits of a poor widow whose only hope resides in her two children. Over and against the creditor, the neighbors represent a kind of social configuration that is communal rather than hierarchically stratified. It is possible to think of them operating out of an ethic of care, rather than an economics of personal gain or self-enhancement.

The creditor and the neighbors in their cameo appearances play key antithetical roles in the story world. The creditor and his plan create the crisis needing resolution. The neighbors and their implied generosity provide the tangible means for the woman to bring about a changed fate for herself and her two children. Faced with the plight of the most vulnerable in ancient Israelite society, these characters represent two courses of action: one grounded in self-interest, defended by legalities, and the other of self-giving, grounded in a communal ethic. In the process, their cameo appearances are not only key to the crisis and resolution in this story. Their cameo appearances also summon readers to dual considerations. Who are the tyrants wielding legalities that further disable the already disenfranchised in our society? And who are the anonymous change-makers, whose small collective acts lift up as worthy the least among us?

NOTES

1. In *Poetics and Interpretation of Biblical Narrative* (Winona Lake, IN: Eisenbrauns, 1994), Adele Berlin defines the category of "type" as a character lacking elaboration and coming off less as a real person and more in accordance with a blueprint of a trait, 31–32.

2. Yael Shemesh, "Elisha and the Miraculous Jug of Oil," *The Journal of Hebrew Scriptures*, vol. 8, no. 4 (2008): 9, notes that the woman does not provide details of her destitute poverty. It is unclear whether the debt stems from her deceased husband or an unpaid loan for which her husband was responsible. It may also stem from her own transaction, since his death, for capital. As an impoverished widow who has nothing in her house, she still has two dependents that she now supports. No doubt her husband's death has played a role in the the worsening of her circumstances.

3. Reading with John Gray, *I & II Kings A Commentary* 2nd Ed. (Philadelphia, PA: Westminster John Knox Press, 1970), who notes the MT *'āsūk* is a hapax legomenon, the meaning "pot" being unattested. The connection with *nāsak* ("to pour") suggests that *'āsuk* may be a corruption of *massāk*, in the proto-Hebraic script, 491, b.

4. Walter Brueggemann portrays creditors as "buzzards circling near-prey," in *1 & 2 Kings, Smyth & Helwys Bible Commentary* (Macon, GA: Smyth & Helwys, 2000), 319.

5. See discussions in Marvin L. Chaney, "Debt Easement in Israelite History and Tradition," in *The Bible and the Politics of Exegesis: Essays in Honor of Norman K. Gottwald on*

His Sixty-fifth Birthday, eds. David Jobling, Peggy L. Day, and Gerald T. Sheppard (Cleveland, OH: The Pilgrim Press, 1991), 127–39; and Kari Latvus, "Debt and Interest in the Hebrew Bible: The Silently Indebted in Ancient Israel and Their Finnish Companions Today," in *Exodus and Deuteronomy*, eds. Athalya Brenner and Gale A. Yee (Minneapolis, MN: Fortress Press, 2012), 287–303.

6. Bruce Chilton, "Debts," in *Interpreter's Dictionary of the Bible* vol. II, 114.

7. Gregory C. Chirichigno, *Debt Slavery in Israel and the Ancient Near East* (Sheffield, UK: Sheffield Academic Press, JSOT Supplemental Series 141, 1993), 123.

8. Ibid, 123.

9. Chaney, "Debt Easement," 136.

10. Marvin L. Chaney, *Peasants, Prophets and Political Economy: The Hebrew Bible and Social Analysis* (Eugene, OR: Cascade Books, 2017), 106.

11. Latvus, 298.

12. A. Graeme Auld, *I & II Kings* (Louisville, KY: Westminster John Knox Press, 1986), 162-63; Burke O. Long, *2 Kings*, The Forms of the Old Testament Literature (Grand Rapids, MI: William B. Eerdmans, 1991), 48–51; G.H. Jones, *1 and 2 Kings*, vol. 2, The New Century Bible Commentary (Grand Rapids, MI: William B. Eerdmans, 1984), 400–4; Iain Provan, *1 and 2 Kings*, New International Biblical Commentary (Peabody, MA: Hendrickson Publishers, 1995), 187–90; Richard Nelson, *First and Second Kings*, Interpretation Commentary (Louisville, KY: John Knox Press, 1987), 170–72.

13. Terence E. Fretheim, *First and Second Kings*, Westminster Bible Companion (Louisville, KY: John Knox Press, 1999), 144–50; Robert Cohn, *2 Kings,* Berit Olam: Studies in Hebrew Narrative & Poetry (Collegeville, MN: Liturgical Press, 2000); Tamis Renteria Hoover, "The Elijah/Elisha Stories: A Socio-cultural Analysis of Prophets and People in Ninth Century B.C.E. Israel," in *Elijah and Elisha in Socio-literary Perspective*, ed. Robert Coote (Atlanta, GA: Scholars Press, 1992), 75–136.

14. Gina Hens-Piazza, *1–2 Kings,* Abingdon Old Testament Commentaries (Nashville, TN: Abingdon Press, 2006), 250–57.

15. Cohn, R., 25.

16. See bell hooks, "Keepers of Hope" in *Teaching Community* (New York: Routledge Press, 2007), 105–16.

17. Lúcás Chan S. J., *Biblical Ethics in the 21st Century: Developments, Emerging Consensus, and Future Directions* (NY: Paulist Press, 2013), 90–92.

18. Ibid., 111.

Chapter Six

Lost in the Telling but Still Present

A Study of Implied Characters in 1 Kings 9:10–14

In the parlance of literary theory, interpreters often speak about implied readers. Years ago, during the rise of reader response criticism, Wolfgang Iser identified the hypothetical figure, whom a given work is designed to address, as the implied reader.[1] Implied readers are to be distinguished from real readers. Real readers reside outside the texts and change from context to context and from generation to generation. Implied readers are suggested or explicated by clues within the text. Subtleties in the narrative or actual indicators in a story suggest the identity of these implied readers. For example, the first-person language of the religious poetry of the Book of Psalms or the Book of Proverbs presumes a faith-filled and God-fearing implied reader, in contrast to any potential real readers, who may or may not be believers. The implied reader is further defined as the reader the author had in mind when the text was composed. Because the implied reader is a construction of the text, Gerald Prince went on to list seven indicators of the implied reader in any composition.[2] Among them, and relevant for this discussion, are the direct references, the indirect reference, and the allusions to the implied reader.

In a similar vein, we can talk about implied characters. Like implied readers, all characters are a construction of the text. Alongside the more well-defined characters of the biblical narratives reside many members of the supporting cast. As we have seen thus far, some of these supporting cast members have more extended roles, significant speaking parts, or are crafted with eccentric features that draw attention to themselves. Others have brief descriptions, recite only a few lines, or are cited only once, while still having an important role to play. But unlike these other members of the supporting cast, implied characters are actually almost invisible and inaudible in these accounts. Yet they still are present and important to the story. Indirect reference to them only hints at their presence, leaving the reader to fill in their silhouettes and bring them to life in the story world. How much the reader knows, or what research the reader enlists, determines the depth and dimension these characters gain in the tale. A reference, "stones being quarried," may sketch an image of hard-working craftsmen with hammers and chisels, laboriously and painstakingly hewing limestone into shaped building blocks. Or a passing mention of "the swindling and tampering with scales" prompts a reader's construction of sly, cunning merchants cheating unsuspecting customers.

Alex Wollech notes that in the narrative distributional matrix, the supporting cast characters are squeezed into tiny narrative spaces.[3] Similarly, in this study, the multitude of implied characters must be compressed into an even tinier space and further delimited if in fact only a hint of them exists in the text. This strategy of displacement of characters also displaces reader's perception of such persons. Any visual or social connection the reader might have with these characters is easily distracted or derailed. Thus, these implied supporting cast members are half visible and half invisible. They are half visible by virtue of an indirect reference that signals their presence in the story. They are half invisible due to the sheer fact that the indirect reference veils either their collective or individual existence. Hence, they are both there and not there in the narrative. We readers unconsciously sketch them into the story, but we rarely focus upon them, and are never really directed by the narrator to pay attention to them.

AN EXAMPLE: 1 KINGS 9:10–14

The account in 1 Kings 9:10–14 recounts a business transaction between two leaders of the ancient Near East during the tenth century: Solomon, King of Israel, and Hiram, King of Phoenicia, Israel's northwest neighbor. At first glance, the two kings seem to be the only characters in this brief text. These five self-contained verses record a trade deal between these two leaders in the course of Solomon's building projects in Jerusalem. The preceding narrative in chapters 5 through 8 provides the context for understanding this deal.[4] In the process of building the temple and his palace, Solomon had secured building materials from Hiram, king of Tyre, Phoenicia's capital (1 Kgs 5:12–18). Some timber had been imported from Lebanon. And, while gold had been used extensively for the furnishing and final decorative treatments of the temple, the source of this metal had not been identified. The present text fills in some of the missing detail as to the source of other timber and precious metal. The passage quickly summarizes Solomon's accomplishment of the foregoing narrative and inscribes an official account of the business transaction that provided the necessary material for these projects. It also adds details missing in earlier accounts.

In the manner suggestive of an impartial record, 1 Kings 9:10–14 opens with a sweeping summary of what the six preceding chapters in 1 Kings 3–8 have detailed. This introduction, "In the twenty years during which Solomon completed the building of the palace and the Temple . . . " (9:10), serves to delimit the time period during which Solomon and Hiram had entered into agreements for the materials required. In lockstep fashion, the record officially inscribes what Hiram provided to Solomon and what, in exchange, Solomon had provided to him. Hiram had supplied Solomon with cedar, cypress timber, and gold, and Solomon had given to Hiram twenty cities in the land of Galilee in exchange (v. 11). All of this serves as background for the only aspect of the record that introduces any narrative tension. Upon receipt of the goods, one of the parties evidently did not think that the agreement was equitable.[5] As the record recounts, "But when Hiram had finally come from Tyre to see the cities that Solomon had given him, they did not please him" (v. 12). And to make the point emphatic and central to the record, the account actually quotes him: "What kind of cities are these that you have given me, my brother?" (v. 13). The passage ends with the addition of an etiological ascription and a clarifying footnote. First, it indicates the territory mortgaged to Hiram is dubbed "Cabul," the meaning of which is a source of ongoing debate. Finally, it notes that Hiram had paid one hundred and twenty talents of gold for these northern cities. Perhaps this hefty sum serves as explanation as to why he was dissatisfied with the trade.

This brief text hardly constitutes a story. Some identify it only as a fragmentary anecdote intended to tell of a "falling out between Solomon and Hiram."[6] Others cast it as a collage of non-chronological pieces of archival material or extracts from the annals of the king.[7] Frequently, this brief text is rendered as a short note belonging to the collection of other miscellaneous items in chapter 9, which merely iterate and amend the previous account in chapters 3 through 8.[8] And as records tend to do, this account rehearses, adds to, and even contradicts detail of what has been narrated in the earlier story.

Whatever form we assign to this brief passage in 1 Kings 9:10–14, this agreement between two kings, Solomon and Hiram, appears fairly ordinary, straightforward, and uncomplicated. At first glance, it could qualify as one of the forms already suggested—archival material, a business record, a fragmentary anecdote. But what appears as a mere ordinary account may not be so innocuous. The official recording here of corporate negotiations between these two front-and-center characters, Solomon and Hiram, hints at another story. It indicates that not only cedar, cypress, and gold were traded between these kings, but cities in northern Israel also entered into the negotiations.

Cities are not just land tracts or vacant, arid acreage. Human settlements comprise cities. These urban constructions imply inhabitants who, this brief record implies, had become collateral in these international transactions. These urban spaces are where people define their relationships, gain their sense of identity, raise their families, claim kinship with a culture, and find meaning and place in a community. Hence, this account of a deal between two monarchs alludes to another account, the untold story of the people of northern Galilee, whose cities are part of a business exchange. The passing detail of these bartered cities hints at other stories embedded here, the stories of the occupants of these towns, whose lives are summarily dismantled as a result of the corporate dealings between two kings. This passing account recording an agreement between two named characters, Solomon and Hiram, rests on the shoulders of the story of an invisible group of implied characters, the inhabitants of these traded towns.

One strategy for studying these more obscure members of the supporting cast involves scrutinizing more extensively the characters that are front and center for what they reveal, by way of similarity with or contrast to the implied characters. Scrutiny of those featured characters, in this case Solomon and Hiram, and their relationship with the implied characters also assists in bringing into full view those half-visible, half-invisible players.

Most of what is recorded in this short passage about Solomon reminds the reader that his building projects constituted the pinnacle of his career. The two main constructions, the palace and the temple, which had already been described in detail in the larger preceding narrative, are in the spotlight again. Our text begins with "At the end of twenty years, in which Solomon had built the two houses, the house of the LORD and the king's house . . . " (v. 10). The temporal notation, "at the end of twenty years," recalls the preceding timeline for the completion of these projects. The construction of the temple took seven years to build (6:38) and the work on the palace lasted thirteen years (7:1). Moreover, this introduction serves as a temporal delimitation. It establishes the duration of business exchanges in the past that occasioned this negotiation between the two kings.

Verse 11 recalls the negotiation between Solomon and Hiram. On the surface, an equitable agreement appears to have taken place. Hiram supplied to Solomon cedar, cypress timber, and gold, and Solomon gave to Hiram cities in Galilee. But the content of the agreement suggests what, perhaps, was not so equitable. Hiram provided Solomon "as much as he desired," while Solomon's provision to Hiram was of limited quantity, "twenty cities in the land of Galilee." Whether this indicates Solomon was a shrewd businessman or willing to negotiate self-serving deals remains to be seen.

Hiram, king of Tyre, had already figured into the larger preceding narrative (1 Kgs. 5:12–18, 7:13–14). The Phoenician ruler had supplied raw materials to Israel since the time of David. During Solomon's tenure, Hiram traded cedar, cypress wood, and skilled labor that Israel needed to advance its material culture. In exchange, Solomon made Israel Phoenicia's granary (1 Kgs 5:12–18). He supplied large quantities of barley, oil, wheat, and wine to Hiram. But the partnership between these two rulers extended beyond these deals. Later, the narrative even notes how Hiram aided Solomon's maintenance of a merchant fleet and cooperated in joint expeditions. Every reference thus far, narrating exchanges between these kings, suggests amicable relations. Hence, verse 11 corroborates and reinforces that impression. It records that Hiram not only supplied Solomon with the raw materials needed for his domestic projects, he also added to Solomon's wealth. In addition to the cedar and cypress that Hiram had provided Solomon, the record now notes that he also provided gold, "as much as he (Solomon) desired" (v. 11).

This is not the only time that the mention of Solomon's affection for gold has occurred. In the preceding report of the furnishing of the temple, the narrative recounts an elaborate tally of objects made of gold. We hear of gold vessels, an altar, a lamp stand, cups, snuffers, basins, and incense dishes, all made of this precious metal. In addition, gold is used to decorate doors, sockets, and altars. Even beyond the gold he receives from Hiram to complete his building project, Solomon's fascination with the precious metal continues. In subsequent narratives, we hear that the queen of Sheba gifts him with gold when she visits (10:2). He acquires gold from traders and merchants, as well as from all the kings of Arabia (10:14). Ships of Tarshish also brought Solomon gold every three years (10:22). And, as the Solomonic narrative draws to a close, we read that his resources for gold spanned the entire world. The kings of the earth brought him presents of gold whenever they came to visit. Hence, Solomon's accumulation of gold may have begun with Hiram but exceeded that king's resources. International relations became a veritable gold mine for Solomon. In the few texts that specify how much gold he accumulated, the amounts are unimaginable.

At the end of our text (v. 14), a footnote adds that Hiram provides Solomon with 120 talents. Though it is difficult to determine exactly the weight of a talent of gold at that time, some suggest a range of 45–130 pounds per talent.[9] Hence, as one scholar calculated, "Hiram paid more than four metric tons of gold for these worthless hamlets."[10] Add that to the weight of other gold Solomon accumulated. In 9:28, the joint fleet of Solomon and Hiram's ships brought him 420 talents of gold. And the gold that came to Solomon in one year after the Queen of Sheba's visit tallied 666 talents. Solomon's use and accumulation of gold appears to be increasing across the years of his reign. But as the Solomonic narrative heads to its conclusion, a most disquieting evaluation of this king will unfold. Texts such as Deuteronomy 17:7 and Proverbs 30:8 portend the danger of accumulating such wealth and precious metal, foreshadowing the indicting judgment that closes this king's legacy. One can only wonder if Solomon misunderstood all that gold as the riches that God had promised this king (3:13, 10:23). Still, Solomon's accumulation of gold was less problematic than what he did to acquire it. For his part, Solomon provided Hiram with twenty cities from the land of Galilee in exchange for those 120 talents of gold.

The question of what constituted Galilee at that time, and more specifically what twenty towns these were, remains unclear. In the broadest terms, Galilee spanned a broad region in the northern portion of the promised land. Traditional representations portray a territory that bordered Lebanon on the north, the Jordan Valley rift in the east and the Jezreel Valley in the south. In Joshua 20:7, the tribe of Naphtali is situated in the land of Galilee. And Isaiah 8:23 identifies the tribal territory of Zebulun and Naphtali as belonging to Galilee.

The detail, "So he called them (the cities) the Land of Cabul, the name they still bear today" (v.13), is a dubious afterthought that closes the record. The phrase reads as if it was added to clarify something about the cities. Jos 19:27 is often cited because it identified a town as Cabul near Acco, a region of the tribe of Asher, located on the western border of the land along the Mediterranean Sea. This would have satisfied Hiram's desire to acquire more coastal towns adjacent to Tyre. However, others read this name as a pun on the possible meaning of Cabul as "fettered," "like nothing."[11] Such an interpretation reads verse 13 as an etiological note that was added to coincide with Hiram's derogatory assessment of the area when he visited the cities (v. 12).

In fact, Hiram's dissatisfaction with the cities introduces the only narrative tension in this short note. Thus, it constitutes the focal point of the brief account. First, the Tyrian ruler visits the cities. "But when Hiram went from Tyre to inspect the cities which Solomon had given him, they did not satisfy him" (v. 12). Then, in the only direct speech in this record, Hiram exclaims his dissatisfaction about what he has received by directing a rhetorical question to Solomon. "What kind of cities are these you have given me, my brother?" (v. 13). While most interpretations focus on the twice-repeated dismay of Hiram in regards to the questionable quality of the territory that Solomon was able to pass off,[12] a further iteration reverberates here and summons our attention. Three times in this short record we hear about cities occupied by Israelite citizens that are being handed over as collateral in this deal with Hiram, king of Phoenicia.

> "*Solomon gave to Hiram twenty cities in the land of Galilee*" (v. 11b)
> "But when Hiram came from Tyre to see *the cities that Solomon had given him,* they did not please him." (v. 12).
> "What kind *of cities are these you have given me,* my brother?" (v. 13)

The first mention of the cities defines them as capital of exchange in the agreement between the two kings. The second time they are mentioned, the cities become the basis of disagreement between the dealing parties. The third time the cities figure into this short note, they are featured as the subject of the only direct speech recorded here. As the focus of an agreement, a disagreement, and finally a point of question as to their quality, the cities rise as central to this record. But a concluding footnote brings a quick end to this momentary impasse. The narrative concludes by reporting that Hiram paid 120 talents for the cities and, in the end, Solomon appears to have sealed the deal. However, the persistent iteration of "the cities of Galilee that Solomon had given to him" should not be missed. The emphasis on how Solomon accomplished this transaction echoes threefold across this narrative. Such repetition suggests something noteworthy: It occasions further consideration by redirecting attention away from these two power-wielding kings toward the cities and their inhabitants, who have become assets for exchange.

Tzvetan Todorov observes that a system of characterization that places characters in a discordant and discrepant relationship with one another can often shape the ideological contours of a narrative.[13] In this brief text, the co-presence of disparate characterization presides. That Solomon can give away these human settlements in Galilee as part of a business transaction sketches a character with unbridled power. That Hiram can visit these cities, evaluate them, and voice his opinion about their lack of acceptability indicates his authoritative position. The inhabitants of the settlements never act or are heard from. They are only implied by the term "cities." They are inferred only by the collective reference suggesting where they reside and, as characters, they remain silent as to their fate at the hands of these monarchs. Such an uneven system of characterization suggests the ideological contours of the type of monarchy operating in the story. Moreover, on three scores, the cities and, by implication, their inhabitants, are deemed unworthy of any attention. First, that Solomon offers to give them away suggests that they are disposable. Second, that Hiram questions the quality of the cities casts a negative shadow over these places that are constituted by and managed by their inhabitants. Finally, the closing etiological note referring to the cities as *Cabul*, a term often assumed to mean "good for nothing," attempts to make right the wrong being foisted upon those who live there.

What further exposition can be given for these "twenty cities of Galilee?" First, the translation of the biblical term (*'irim*) for "cities" cultivates misunderstanding. The English word "city" does not describe the sociological construct that the biblical text references with the Hebrew word. There is no word, in fact, in English or the European languages that adequately conveys the concept of the *'irim*. Some translate it "town" or "village" but, at best, it needs to be rendered as "human settlement." Moreover, the term *'ir* (pl. *'im*) does not designate anything uniform in terms of a physical profile.[14]

The size of an *'ir* in biblical Syria and Palestine was not measured in miles but in acres. The average Hebrew Palestinian city in pre-Hellenistic times is only twenty to thirty acres, at best. For example, Jerusalem, during Solomon's reign, was considered very grand because it spanned approximately thirty acres.[15]

The population density of "city" in the pre-Hellenistic era was on average eighty to a hundred persons per acre. Describing cities in terms of such demographics necessarily prompts thinking of cities in terms of people. It suggests that the number of people dwelling in the biblical cities was approximately 2,000–3,000.[16] Such a size and occupation matches something close to a very small town or village in modern times. It is also noteworthy that many of these "cities" were associated with surrounding fields or land tracts outside the city walls (Num 35:5). Though the relationship between urban and rural was once thought to be dichotomous, recent cultural studies now conclude the opposite. In fact, the biblical "city" was a dependent construct. Various landscapes beyond the city limits were considered parts of the coordinated whole. The city depended upon the immediately surrounding rural life for meat, milk, animals, skins, wool. And the rural surrounding population depended upon the city for a place to sell their crops and for processed goods.[17] Walled cities provided refuge for those outside the wall. An alarm would alert people in the fields to take cover within the city walls.[18] Even with the growth of a monarchic society and the rise of its "cities," Israelite society retained its predominantly agricultural and pastoral bases. No radical dichotomy separated cities and their inhabitants from the surrounding agricultural tracts and their inhabitants. A distinct interdependence between urban and rural presided and, in fact, is reflected in the religious practices and beliefs of the cities, especially those of the Canaanites. Hence, giving away twenty cities of Galilee disrupted more than the inhabitants of these human settlements. The whole rural population would also be affected. The social networks and interdependence with cities, with which rural communities were engaged, would also be dismantled.

But Solomon's deeding the twenty cities to Hiram disrupts more than the urban and rural networks of relationship, social exchanges, and economic interdependence upon which people's livelihoods counted. Each inhabitant's identity also would come under assault. In ancient Israel, a person's identity stemmed from two compulsory markers: kinship and homeplace. In the Book of Ruth, Boaz takes Ruth as wife before the assembly of witnesses. But he does something more. He also ensures something very important for Mahlon, Ruth's deceased husband. By taking Ruth as wife, Boaz makes it possible that "the name of the dead man will not be cut off from among his kin and from the gate of his homeplace" (Ruth 4:9–10).[19]

There is frequent debate as to whether kinship and homeplace are of equal standing in ancient Israel. Kinship tends to be viewed as the older priority.[20]

In the post-exilic period, although kinship terms were still used, a person was apt to be marked and identified first by homeplace. Still, the persistence of kinship affiliation into the first century C.E. is quite remarkable. In Romans 11:1, Paul is identified as from the tribe of Benjamin. The notions of both kinship and homeplace are complex, evolve and, thus, change in meaning over the centuries and among different groups of people.

Kinship is a much explored concept concerning the understanding of ancient Israel. In the broadest terms, kinship refers to both blood ties and social connections. While often socially constructed, kinship is one of the most fundamental ways people define themselves. In ancient Israel, a person was a member of a household (*bet 'ab*), a clan or heritage (*mishpah*), and a tribe (*mateh*). The household was patriarchal, identified with the father figure of that family. It often included several generations who dwelt together or in close proximity. This extended family was the basic unit of ownership of property, land cultivation, and pastoral responsibilities. The clan was thought to consist of several of these extended families living in nearby areas. Some part of the clan might live in more urban settings, while the other members could work the land tracts associated with this group. The members of the clan were interlocked by marriage, employment, and communal benefit from common ownership of the land. There appears to be a high correspondence between the parameters of urban settlements (so-called cities) and the radius of a clan. Clans used the language of kinship to describe the social ties between members of that group. Real and fictional shared pasts and ancestry identified the clan members as descendants of a common ancestor. Tribal identity was a more fluid and vague social category. Division and relations were far more complex, and the tribe tended to be more territorial than ancestral in nature. Especially during the monarchical period, tribal relations and divisions changed from time to time. In establishing a more centralized government, Solomon sought to disrupt these ties. He redistricts the land and settles governors over each district, which also serves to disrupt earlier cooperative local identity collectives (1 Kgs 4:7–19). Still, each of these memberships—household, clan, and tribe—contributed to one's place, rule, and identity in the community to which a person belonged. In particular, these memberships also insured the well-being of the individual in terms of the interdependence in which one's livelihood was grounded. In addition, these social affiliations defined and verified one's identity if an individual traveled outside the confines of the family or the clan as someone other than an "outsider" or "foreigner." For example, they would identify as members of the household of Jacob or of the tribe of Benjamin.[21]

Giving away cities included severing family and clan ties that defined identity and disrupted the social and biological datum by which people understood themselves. Cut off from the networks that constituted their standing in these various social groups, their own self-understanding was made liminal. Kinship ties of mother, father, brothers, sisters, sons, daughters, in-laws, and so on, in extended families and surrounding regions would be threatened. The terms by which one understood one's self and one's relationship with a core group incurred an interruption that lasted forever. More significantly, the cooperative infrastructure upon which sustenance and livelihood depended disappeared.

Unlike kinship, which described one's ties to other individuals or collective groups, homeplace defines a person's tie to land. The land in Israel was more than just property. It was the sign of the covenant that bound a people to a deity. It carried ancestral ties, about which people rehearsed their past and that of their families. The story of Naboth's refusal to hand over his land to King Ahab (1 Kgs 21) because it was his ancestral heritage is illustrative. This mortgaging of land by the Solomonic government denies recognition of all these dimensions of meaning ascribed to land in Israel. The territory of the northern kingdom constituted historic homelands. Exchanging this property for gold or for building materials flies in the face of Israel's story of salvation, the core of which narrated the granting of land to this people. In the most elemental terms, bartering the land ignores the rights of the men and women who live there and made it their home.

Besides the devastating impact on whole groups of people residing in these cities and the surrounding regions, the loss of land is particularly ominous on another score. The divine threat occurring in Solomon's dream in the preceding verses (1 Kgs 9:11–13) reminds the king that the punishment for apostasy is the loss of land.[22] Yet the loss of land pales in comparison to the consequence of this loss. Focusing upon the loss of land obscures the real expenditure—people's lives, identity, community, and future. Loss of land granted for the livelihood of God's people threatens that well-being.

As the story narrates that the twenty cities become part of the Tyrian domain under Hiram's rule, it does invite the reader to pause and imagine the fate of the inhabitants living in these urban centers and the surrounding rural areas. Whether they remain in the cities now newly acquired by Tyre or become refugees in other parts of Israel, the life they once knew has disappeared. If they remain in the cities, their way of being is jarred. They go to bed Israelites and wake up in the morning discovering that they are Phoenicians living in Tyre. They now live under a foreign government that does not know them or perhaps even recognize their rights. The means by which they made a living or held a place in the community may no longer be legitimate in this new society, whose economic and social structure redefines the very terms of their livelihood. Even the claims that they had on buildings, properties, or other securities now go unrecognized under this new governance. Despite their lifelong occupation of this territory once known as a part of Israel, they now would become foreigners on what had been their own soil. Their identity with Yahweh which, according to their religious traditions, tied them to settlement in this land is also summarily dismantled. Hence, the disruption had religious consequences. It may require that their livelihood and thus allegiance whether accepted willingly or now forced depended upon their allegiance to the Baals. Even with years of cultural assimilation that the future would require, these past inhabitants of Israelite cities will continue to be the newcomers or outsiders for generations to come. As outsiders, they might be required to take up the least favorable employment, despite their knowledge, successes, and accomplishments of the past. These may well not be recognized in this new national setting. This is not just an ancient phenomenon. Their story and fate illuminates the struggles of communities of our own time. Peoples whose whole land or even parts of their country have been confiscated by other international powers often become landless migrants on what was once their own acreage. They are reduced to menial jobs when previously they had succeeded in skilled professions. Often they end up working as tenants on land that had once belonged to their ancestors. Families are separated by work assignments, by the need to go wherever work can now be found.

For those who flee the cities in order to remain in Israel, their fate is equally insecure. They now live in their country as refugees or as subjects of others' charity. They remain governed by the Solomonic administration that had displaced them and caused such disruption in their lives. If they are able to resettle on a piece of land to which they have no ancestral claim, they will always live under the potential threat that they can be driven off the land again. One need only think of people today to better grasp the consequences of displacement. Where they live, build their houses, and set up their schools is constantly being disrupted with redistricting of land. Extended families are barely established in a new settlement when new boundaries, fence lines, or even walls are established that separate these kinship groups. They are refugees among their own people, often living in temporary camps, waiting for assignment to a place or space to occupy. Like many people today, the occupants of these Galilean cities likely became refugees on their own soil. As displaced persons, they are subject to the effects of trauma that the loss of homeplace, kinship, and livelihood conjure. They, who once cared for the "orphan, sojourner, and widow," now become the orphan, sojourner, and widow, who must depend upon others for sustenance. The self-reliance that grants self-respect, integrity, and identity is stripped away. Identification with a household or urban community or with a tribal or ancestral past has disappeared. Hence, whether as occupants of towns now under Tyrian rule or as displaced persons who remain in Israel, it is defensible to think that this forfeiting of land threatens, if not destroys, the economic, social, and cultural well-being of every person once resident of these bartered cities.

CONCLUSION

Due to its lack of drama and thick plot, the account in 1 Kings 9:10–14 can be easily bypassed. Commentators have given it significant attention in their analyses primarily due to unresolved historical and textual matters. The question of whether the deal between Solomon and Hiram was during or after the completion of the building projects has garnered the discussion and debate. The meaning of the naming of the cities "Cabal," exactly what cities these were, as well as why Hiram was displeased have all invited conjecture. And whether or not Solomon was indeed an entrepreneuring businessman or a ruler with an empty treasury has been argued as the reason for this text. Yet few have ever attended to the real tragedy sketched in this brief record. Indeed, some have acknowledged that trading Israelite land, the gift associated with the covenant, was problematic.[23] But little if any attention has been given to the matter of "whole populations viewed as pawns of a royal wish"[24] and being traded for building materials and gold. The implied inhabitants of these cities are the muted multitudes whose character and role are passed over in most inquiries about these verses. Their fate is never considered, even as the most remote background of this account. In a record about a negotiation between kings that disrupts and destabilizes their lives, these persons are present only by implication. Thus, they never are able to narrate the consequences of this deal for them. Their eventual status as dislocated persons in that society coincides with their silent and concealed status in the narrative. Despite their characterization as mute and invisible, their presence, when focused upon by attentive readers, complicates what otherwise appears as a harmless passing record.

Fixing upon these implied characters reminds us that every story is more than it appears. Even one very brief story speaks of other stories. Moreover, attention to these least visible of the supporting cast nudges us beyond the complacency and narrowness characteristic of reading practices. It emancipates us from the caste system of the narrative and invites us to see those whose story, though present, is obscured. Further, a more inclusive way of reading this text summons us to greater cognizance of the effects that our own deals and decisions have upon each other. That every agreement reaping an excess of gains for one or two individuals, parties, or even countries always has some effects upon others who are often unseen and inaudible. And when those decisions are between powerful parties, the outcome for other large groups of people can also be very powerful, even devastating. Dwelling upon the implied characters in this story cultivates a vision to see their counterparts in our own surroundings, people who reap the difficult consequences of similar bargains between those with authority, between governments, or between global organizations. Training our attention upon these multitudes fosters sensitivity for such persons and makes visible what has been unseen. Recognition of the nameless, silent populations is indeed only a first step, but it is a necessary one in the effort to reverse their fate.

NOTES

1. Wolfgang Iser, "The Reading Process: A Phenomenological Approach," in *Reader-Response Criticism: From Formalism to Post-Structuralism*, ed. Jane P. Tompkins (Baltimore, MD: Johns Hopkins University Press, 1980), 50–70.

2. Gerald Prince, "Introduction to the Study of the Narratee," *in Reader-Response Criticism: From Formalism to Post-Structuralism*, ed. Jane P. Tompkins. (Baltimore, MD: Johns Hopkins University Press, 1980), 7–25.

3. Alex Woloch, *The One and the Many: Minor Characters and the Space of the Protagonist in the Novel* (Princeton, NJ: Princeton University Press, 2003), 152.

4. Richard Nelson, *First and Second Kings*, Interpretation: A Bible Commentary (Louisville, KY: John Knox Press, 1987), 62–63.

5. Contra Jeffrey Kuan, "Third Kingdoms 5.1 and Israelite-Tyrian Relations During the Reign of Solomon," *Journal for the Study of the Old Testament* 46 (1990): 39, who argues that Hiram's displeasure may have been due to Solomon running out of resources to pay tribute, rather than any dissatisfaction with the cities.

6. Burke Long, *1 Kings:* The Forms of the Old Testament Literature (Grand Rapids, MI: Wm. B. Eerdmans Publishing Co., 1984), 112.

7. J. Robinson, *The First Book of Kings* (London: Cambridge University Press, 1972), 115, and Simon J. DeVries, *1 Kings*, Word Biblical Commentary (Waco, TX: Word Books, Publisher, 1985), 131.

8. Martin Mulder, *1 Kings: Volume 1: 1 Kings 1–11.* (Leuven, Belgium: Peeters, 1998), 472.

9. John Gray, *I & II Kings: A Commentary*, Old Testament Library (Philadelphia: Westminster, 1963), 224.

10. Nelson, 63–64.

11. Much discussion surrounds the meaning and, therefore, the significance of the term Cabul (*kābûl*) in this account. Etymological explanations that suggest translating it "mortgaged" are forwarded by Gray, 224; Gwilym H. Jones, *1 and 2 Kings*, 2 vols. New Century Bible (Grand Rapids, MI: Eerdmans, 1984), 214. James Montgomery and Henry Synder Gehman in *A Critical and Exegetical Commentary on the Books of Kings*, International Critical Commentary (Edinburgh: T & T Clark. 1951), 205, render it "March-land." Iain W. Provan, in *1 and 2 Kings*, New International Bible Commentary on the Old Testament (Peabody, MA: Hendrickson, 1995), 88, translates it "fettered." Others propose the possibility that "Cabul represents an auditory corruption of 'boundary' (*gābûl*), as attested in the LXX." See Jerome Walsh, *1 Kings*, Berit Olam: Studies in Hebrew Narrative & Poetry (Collegeville, MN: Liturgical Press, 1996), 121 n.1, and Eric Seibert, *Subversive Scribes and the Solomonic Narrative: A Rereading of I Kings 1–11* (New York: T&T Clark Library of Biblical Studies, 2003), 174 n.72, who also notes the attempts by some to identify Cabul with an actual location near Acco (Jos 19:27).

12. Provan, 84-85; Walsh, 120–21; and Gina Hens-Piazza, *1–2 Kings*, Abingdon Old Testament Commentaries (Nashville: Abingdon Press, 2006), 90–91.

13. Tzvetan Todorov, *Qu'est-ce c' est la structuralisme* (Paris: Editions du Seuil, 1973), 72.

14. See Michael Patrick O'Connor, "The Biblical Notion of the City" *in Constructions of Space II: The Biblical City and Other Imagined Spaces*, eds. John Berquist and Claudia Camp (New York: T&T Clark Library of Biblical Studies, 2008), 18–39.

15. Philip King, *Anchor Bible Dictionary*, 3rd edition, ed. David Noel Freedman (New York: Bantam Doubleday Group, 1992), 753.

16. O'Connor, 30.

17. Lester Grabbe and Robert Haak, eds., "Introduction and Overview," in *'Every City Shall Be Forsaken': Urbanism and Prophecy in Ancient Israel and the Near East.* JSOT Supplement Series (Sheffield, UK: Sheffield Academic Press Ltd., 2001), 32–33.

18. Frank Frick, *The City in Ancient Israel* (Missoula, MT: Scholars Press, 1977), 93.

19. O'Connor notes this example as well as acknowledges that the "passage is famously difficult in terms of the book of Ruth, since the raising up of the dead man's name does not happen" in the story, 25.

20. Ibid.

21. See Joshua 7:16–18, where all three of these designations of identity reside in one story.

22. The egregiousness of Solomon's handing over the land in this transaction has been noted by several scholars. See Siebert, 177; Walsh, 122; Hens-Piazza, 93; and Jung Ju Kang, *The Persuasive Portrayal of Solomon in I Kings 1–11* (Bern, Switzerland: Peter Lang, 2003), 199.

23. Walsh, 122; Walter Brueggemann, *1 & 2 Kings,* Smyth & Helwys Bible Commentary (Macon, GA: Smyth & Helwys, 2000), 123; Seibert, 176; and Rob Barrett, *Disloyalty and Destruction: Religion and Politics in Deuteronomy and the Modern World* (New York: T&T Clark Library of Biblical Studies, 2009), 226.

24. Brueggemann, 123, and Hens-Piazza, 93.

Conclusion

In this study, the proposed taxonomy employed to group these numerous members of the supporting cast—"complementary character," "bit-part character," "cameo appearance character," "implied character"—is not based upon a character's quality or importance. Rather, it attends primarily to an assessment of other factors: the amount of narrative space occupied by characters, whether they are assigned direct discourse, how much they actually have to say, as well as their visibility. Such criteria intend that the boundaries of each grouping are not rigid. Instead, these categories court a flexibility regarding to which group each character might be assigned. These assignments have much to do with a reader's own assessment and perception of a character's role in the story. For example, visibility itself is a perspectival judgment. So, a character such as the cannibal mother in 2 Kings 6:23–31, who in this study is analyzed as a "complementary character," might easily be thought of as a "bit-part character" by some readers. Or the servant girl and the servants in 2 Kings 5:1–19, because of their brief description and limited speaking parts, are discussed as examples of "bit-part" characters. Yet, the servant girl's influence endures throughout the story. She and the other servants have such an influential role in Naaman's cure and conversion. Thus, because they have a staying power beyond their actual presence in the narrative, some might consider them "complementary characters." Therefore, the parameters of these categories are not fixed but fluid.

The four groupings promote recognition and organization, rather than imposing strict categorizations or limiting definitions to these numerous members of the supporting cast. Categories are proposed so each and every member of the supporting cast would have a designation and, thus, a way to be acknowledged. Further, these four groups are intended as alternative nomenclature for the previous analytical categories in order to resist diminishing labels such as "minor character," which discourage consideration of the importance any character might have in a story.

Among the many factors that have affected how we read texts, the influence of feminist studies, postcolonial studies, and shifts in literary studies have played particular roles in encouraging such attention to the supporting cast. Feminist scholars continue to focus upon and feature the stories of both the women who are front and center in biblical narrative, as well as those women characters whose stories are embedded there but have never been acknowledged.[1] Postcolonial theory has also informed biblical interpretation in a matter that lifts up and makes visible previously unattended individual characters, or whole populations, in the texts. Previously colonized in the social world of the story, obscured by the dominance of protagonist, or often demoted by analytical categories of interpreters, these characters have been brought out of the shadows in stories that obscured them by postcolonial interpretations.[2] In addition, new trends in literary studies have influenced how we read and who we see in texts. The study of character has come to dominate and even take precedence over previous concentrations on plot. The recognition of reader response criticism of readers' participation, in not only the reception but in the composition of the story, has proved most essential.[3] The influence of postmodernism has raised questions about these narratives, bringing these supporting cast characters and their seemingly tiny roles into the foreground. Cultural studies have illuminated the unnoticed dimensions of stories, where hints of these supporting cast characters and their stories reside. New Historicism also lifts up the presence and importance of a narrative's supporting cast by shifting attention away from what is central and toward what resides on the periphery and by asking questions about what was previously not interrogated in these stories.[4] Hence, this study of the supporting cast rests upon the foundation laid by feminist studies, postcolonial studies, and the new horizons pursued in literary studies.

That all four character analyses taken up in chapters 3 through 6 in this project derive from texts in the Books of Kings also has an historical backdrop. Several years ago, the influence of feminist studies, postcolonial projects, and shifts in literary studies stirred a genuine unrest in this author during the completion of a fairly traditional commentary project on the books of Kings. That disquiet seeded the germination of this study. The unmistakable focalization on kings and their activities in these historical narratives constantly courted looking past a plethora of other characters that resided in the same stories. Midway through the two books, the Elisha/Elijah narratives (1 Kgs 17–2 Kgs 9) seemed, at first, to offer a brief reprieve. But instead, these two prophets, rather than kings, now commanded center stage, and the multitudes of other characters still remained on the sidelines. Whether riveted upon prophets or kings, the chapters of 1 and 2 Kings all seemed to unfold on the backs of a large cadre of characters, about whom little was featured and who invited little attention in the available research. These supporting cast members rarely received mention in the interpretive literature. For example, when the laborers for Solomon's building projects (1 Kgs 9:15–21), the older men who advised Rehoboam (1 Kgs 12:6–7), the nurse of King Joash (2 Kgs 11:2–3), the elders gathered in Elisha's house (2 Kgs 6:32), or the captain pleading before Elijah (2 Kgs 2:13–14) are cited in the text, such references to them typically are understood in the service of forwarding or enhancing the story surrounding the king or the prophet. In keeping with the analytical categories of traditional literary theory, these various and thinly sketched individuals usually are relegated to the domain of "minor characters." Their status is often thought to be subsidiary. As adjuncts, they simply verify the social position, the office, or the authority of the main characters in whose service they function. Some do not even qualify as "minor characters," so little is said of them. They are often viewed as the expected human scenery populating a ruler's milieu or as the necessary public witness required to authorize a religious official's power. Hence, the so-called major characters that command interpretive attention hover over and obscure the presence and significance of these supporting cast members. The major characters are thought to dominate, occupying centrality in both the story and in interpretation.

However, this study raises questions about the very notion of centrality itself. Supporting cast members that have been relegated to the periphery in both the text and in interpretation have emerged here as significant, even central, to the development of the tale. In 2 Kings 4:1–7, two cameo appearance characters are key to both the crisis and the resolution of the plot. The creditor and his threat to take the widow's two children constituted the crisis about which the story revolves. And while the prophet's intervention, the widow's initiative, and the children's cooperation contribute to the successful outcome, these best-laid plans could not have succeeded without the cooperation of the neighbors. According to the prophet's instructions to the woman, the cooperation of "all of the neighbors" was required. Both the creditor and the neighbors appear only once in the story and then immediately disappear from the tale. They have no speaking parts or receive any description. Yet, the crisis of the story and its resolution depend upon them. Each had a story to tell that was implied in the narrative and, with attention fixed upon them, their stories emerged. They became significant and central to the storyline and its interpretation.

Some years ago, Jonathan Culler wrote, "What is the center if the marginal can become central?"[5] Culler's rhetorical question suggests that centrality is largely a matter of point of view. And point of view is not confined to the author or even the text. The reader also brings to the table a point of view. So, the notion of center itself becomes qualified. In this study, what had been defined as marginal or trivial has, in fact, proved to be important and even vital. And what is important and vital to a story might well share the status of central. So, it follows that what is deemed major or minor also involves perspectival judgments. A character typically defined as major could turn out to be of less centrality, or significance, when compared with the role of a supporting cast member. What this indicates is that all characters really begin on equal footing. Some are granted more narrative space and airtime in a story. But that does not necessarily grant them automatic centrality or an importance that obscures the centrality or importance of other less visible characters.

As in texts, so too in life itself. Some persons are well known due to media attention, the public offices they occupy, or the featured contributions they make to a society. But for each of these celebrated individuals there exist counterparts whose self-sacrifice or game-changing contributions go unseen and unacknowledged but who also have equal impact, or sometimes even more influence, upon the well-being of society. Whether we see and acknowledge them has to do, to some degree, with how we read texts like the Bible, and the reverse is true as well.

Indeed, the study of the supporting cast does have its aesthetically satisfying yield. However, the importance of the enterprise is much more than a merely artistic interest. The examination of the supporting cast may add further dimensions to our moral paradigm. Such a study discloses new examples of who is virtuous or who is the victim of not only explicit but also of subtle or unrecognized violence. This focus unveils persons of valor and integrity or those who have been denied choice in their lives. However, not all supporting cast members are praiseworthy or establish new moral benchmarks. Some are morally culpable and are the doers of violence themselves. For example, the cameo appearance of the "creditor" in 2 Kings 4:1–7 created the crisis which unfolded in the story. He intended to collect on the outstanding debt of the widow by confiscating her two children. At first glance, he may appear to be acting within his legal rights. But further exposition of the sociohistorical information that thickens his character reveals him as someone willing to devastate further a widow's status in a society where she is already especially vulnerable. By contrast, the neighbors, though obscured and delimited in the narrative, prove to be the counterforce that acts in the interest of the widow. And though their action remains unnarrated, and thus invisible, the evidence of the story suggests they responded wholeheartedly. Their unsung generosity gives us pause, inviting consideration of who in our own surroundings are the practitioners of unrecognized kindness who, perhaps, support our own well-being. Hence, this study of those deemed peripheral to the story is often a reflection of what proves to be true in life but goes unacknowledged.

The study of these supporting cast characters is not a campaign to champion a minority group, per se, nor should it be interpreted as character rescue work. Rather, once begun, it is intrinsically appealing, in part because it builds our own character. We learn about ourselves as we study others who are both similar and dissimilar to ourselves. We find characters whose strength and courage we identify with, like the servants in 2 Kings 5:1–19. At times these supporting cast characters may afford a glance at dimensions of ourselves that might otherwise go unseen. They can act as mirrors, whose reflections help us to better understand ourselves. Or a study of these other characters may inspire us. Like the diplomacy and audacity of the servant girl in that same story, they may nudge us beyond our fears or complacencies. They may become a daily reminder of what we want to be. But study of the supporting cast should not be romanticized. Some of these characters can also repel us. At first glance, the cannibal mother invites such a response. At times, such a negative reaction to a character is justified. But as the study of this pathetic character disclosed, her apparent status as a doer of violence revealed her to be a victim of violence, afflicting her as well as large segments of a society. The more we learned about her "story from below," the more our indicting sentiments may have shifted to the political and religious powers responsible for such systematic violence. Such a change in our own perception gives us pause before others whom we may be quick to judge. Instead, we may be encouraged to take a longer, more informed look and recognize the complexity of others' lives, which may make their misdeeds understandable or, at least, more difficult to condemn.

Strangely, some of the most compelling insights about ourselves and what is possible for our lives might be prompted by those individuals whom we have been conditioned to ignore, whether in life or in texts. We realize this when we study the supporting cast because of an uncomfortable pang of recognition. These characters, both in their positive and negative attributes, often are a lot like who we are. Fixing attention on these characters offers not only insights about ourselves but expands our perspective on the world in which we live. New heroes emerge. The self-sacrifice of quiet multitudes becomes visible. The occurrence of subtle, but nevertheless real injustices may be revealed. Covert practitioners of virtue and even of violence may start to be recognized. Hence, the supporting cast invites recognition and interpretation because they matter.

We have been discussing that how we read important religious and cultural texts, such as the Bible, influences how we read the texts of our world. And that influence enhances our own self-knowledge, deepens our understanding of one another and, perhaps occasionally, even cultivates the development of new empathies. So, the inherent challenge lies before us. We can just read, or we can read in a way that is more just, more inclusive, and more democratized. Our reading can be an act of complacency, attending only to where the narrative navigates our attention. Or, our reading can be an act of resistance, refusing to fix our gaze only where the narrative directs us. Our reading can support the caste system of the narrative, or we can read and learn from the supporting cast. At the same time, we remind ourselves that how we read, who we inquire about, what questions we ask are not unrelated to the way in which we live. Thus, reading in ways that make us grapple with the broadest range of characters in biblical narrative makes such reading more than a private spiritual practice or self-satisfying aesthetic exercise. It has the potential to fashion us into people more willing to acknowledge our differences, more able to work across lines that divide us, and more determined to resist polarization among ourselves—whether in our cities, our country, across our various religious traditions, and in our world. In the end, such a potential yield seems like sufficient justification for the study of this vast and motley array of characters, referred to here as the supporting cast.

NOTES

1. In addition to the numerous articles and full-length studies by feminist scholars since the early 1970s, two longer works that attend to women characters in the biblical traditions are noteworthy. See Carol A. Newsom, Sharon H. Ringe, and Jacqueline E. Lapsley, eds. *Women's Bible Commentary*, 3rd edition, Revised and Updated (Louisville, KY: Westminster John Knox Press, 2012); Luise Schottroff and Marie-Therese Wacker, eds. *Feminist Biblical Interpretation: A Compendium of Critical Commentary on the Books of the Bible and Related Literature* (Grand Rapids, MI: Eerdmans, 2012).

2. Among the many examples of postcolonial studies on biblical texts, as an example, see R. S. Sugirtharajah, *The Postcolonial Biblical Reader* (Hoboken, NJ: Wiley-Blackwell, 2005).

3. The collection of essays in Jane Tompkins, ed., *Reader Response Criticism: From Formalism to Post-Structuralism* (Baltimore, MD: Johns Hopkins University Press, 1980) still serves as one of the most comprehensive overviews of the development of reader response criticism.

4. See Gina Hens-Piazza, *The New Historicism: Guides to Biblical Scholarship* (Minneapolis: Augsburg Press, 2002).

5. Jonathan Culler, *On Deconstruction: Theory and Criticism after Structuralism* (Ithaca, NY: Cornell University Press, 1982), 140.

Bibliography

Abrams, M. H. *The Mirror and the Lamp: Romantic Theory and the Critical Tradition.* London/Oxford: Oxford University Press, 1953.
Adam, A. K. M. *What Is Postmodern Biblical Criticism?* Minneapolis: Fortress Press, 1995.
Alter, Robert. *Ancient Israel: The Former Prophets: Joshua, Judges, Samuel, Kings : A Translation with Commentary.* New York: W. W. Norton & Company, 2014.
———. *The Art of Biblical Narrative.* New York: Basic Books, Inc., Publishers, 1981.
Ashcroft, Bill, Gareth Griffiths and Helen Tiffin, eds. *The Post-Colonial Reader,* 2nd ed. London: Routledge, 2004.
Auerbach, Erich. *Mimesis: The Representation of Reality in Western Literature.* Princeton, NJ: Princeton University Press, 1953.
Auld, A. Graeme. *I & II Kings.* Louisville, KY: Westminster John Knox Press, 1986.
Bailie, Gil. *Violence Unveiled: Humanity at the Crossroads.* New York: Crossroads, 1995.
Bakhtin, Michel. *The Dialogic Imagination: Four Essays,* ed. Michael Holquist. Translated by Caryl Emerson and Michael Holquist. Austin: University of Texas Press, 1982.
Barrett, Rob. *Disloyalty and Destruction: Religion and Politics in Deuteronomy and the Modern World.* New York: T&T Clark Library of Biblical Studies, 2009.
Barthes, Roland. *S/Z: An Essay.* New York: Hill and Wang, 1974.
Berlin, Adele. *Poetics and Interpretation of Biblical Narrative.* Winona Lake, IN: Eisenbrauns, 1994.
Booth, Wayne C. *The Rhetoric of Fiction.* Chicago: University of Chicago Press, 1983.
Boyarin, Daniel. *Carnal Israel: Reading Sex in Talmudic Culture,* The New Historicism: Studies in Cultural Poetics, vol. 25. Berkeley: University of California Press, 1993.
Brooks, Geraldine. *March.* London: Penguin Press, 2004.
Brown, Francis, S. R. Driver, and C. A. Briggs, eds. *A Hebrew and English Lexicon of the Old Testament .* Oxford, UK: Clarendon, 1907.
Brown, Pamela, and Don Tuzin, eds. *The Ethnography of Cannibalism.* Washington, DC: Society for Psychological Anthropology, 1983.
Brueggemann, Walter. *1 & 2 Kings : Smyth & Helwys Bible Commentary.* Macon, GA: Smyth & Helwys Publishing Incorporated, 2000.
———. *2 Kings,* Knox Preaching Guides. Atlanta, GA: John Knox, 1982.
Cambridge Advanced Learner's Dictionary & Thesaurus, https://dictionary.cambridge.org/us/dictionary/english/bit-part.
Camp, Claudia. "The Female Sage in Ancient Israel and the Biblical Wisdom Literature," in *The Sage in Ancient Israel.* Eds., J. Gammie and Leo Purdue. Winona Lake, IN: Eisenbrauns, 1990.

———. "1 and 2 Kings." In *The Women's Bible Commentary*, 3rd ed., eds. Carol Newsom and Sharon Ringe. Louisville, KY: Westminster John Knox, 1992.

Chan, Lúcás. *Biblical Ethics in the 21st Century: Developments, Emerging Consensus, and Future Directions*. New York: Paulist Press, 2013.

Chan, Lúcás, James F. Keenan, and Ronaldo Zacharias. *The Bible and Catholic Theological Ethics*. Maryknoll, NY: Orbis Books, 2017.

Chaney, Marvin L. "Debt Easement in Israelite History and Tradition." *The Bible and the Politics of Exegesis : Essays in Honor of Norman K. Gottwald on His Sixty-fifth Birthday*. Eds. David Jobling, Peggy L. Day, and Gerald T. Sheppard. Cleveland, OH: The Pilgrim Press, 1991.

———. *Peasants, Prophets and Political Economy: The Hebrew Bible and Social Analysis*. Eugene, OR: Cascade Books, 2017.

Chatman, Seymour. *Story and Discourse: Narrative Structure in Fiction and Film*. Ithaca, NY: Cornell University Press, 1978.

Chirichigno, Gregory C. *Debt Slavery in Israel and the Ancient Near East*. Sheffield, UK: Sheffield Academic Press, JSOT Supplemental Series 141, 1993.

Cogan, Mordechai, and Hayim Tadmor. *II Kings*, Anchor Bible Commentary. New York: Doubleday, 1988.

Cohn Eskenazi, Tamar, and Tikva Frymer-Kensky. *The Book of Ruth*. JPS Commentary Series. Philadelphia: The Jewish Publication Society, 2011.

Cohn, Robert L. "Form and Perspective in 2 Kings V." *VT* 31 (1983): 174.

———. *2 Kings Berit Olam: Studies in Hebrew Narrative and Poetry*. Collegeville, MN: The Liturgical Press, 2000.

Culler, Jonathan. *On Deconstruction: Theory and Criticism after Structuralism*. Ithaca, NY: Cornell University Press, 1982.

de Certeau, Michel. "Reading as Poaching." In *The Practice of Everyday Life*. Minneapolis: University of Minnesota Press, 1984.

Exum, J. Cheryl. *Plotted, Shot, and Painted: Cultural Representation of Biblical Women*. Sheffield, UK: Sheffield Academic Press, 1996.

——— and Stephen Moore, eds. *Biblical Studies/Cultural Studies*. Sheffield, UK: Sheffield Academic Press Ltd., 1998.

Fish, Stanley. *Is There a Text in this Class? The Authority of Interpretive Communities*. Cambridge, MA: Harvard University Press, 1980.

Floriani, Ana. "Negotiating What Counts: Roles and Relationships, Texts and Contexts, Content and Meaning." *Linguistics and Education* 5 (1993): 241-74.

Forster, E. M. *Aspects of the Novel*. New York: Harcourt & Brace, 1927.

Fretheim, Terence. *Deuteronomistic History*. Nashville: Abingdon Press, 1983.

———. *First and Second Kings*. Louisville, KY: Westminster John Knox Press, 1999.

Frick, Frank. *The City in Ancient Israel* . Missoula, MT: Scholars Press, 1977.

Galef, David. *The Supporting Cast—a Study of Flat and Minor Characters*. University Park: Pennsylvania State University Press, 1993.

Gallagher, Catherine, and Stephen Greenblatt. *Practicing New Historicism*. Chicago: The University of Chicago Press, 2000.

Garvey, James. "Characterization in the Narrative," *Poetics* 7 (1978): 63–78.

Gass, William. *Fiction and the Figures of Life*. Jaffrey, NH: David R. Godine, 1978.

Grabbe, Lester, and Robert Haak, eds. "Introduction and Overview." In *'Every City Shall Be Forsaken': Urbanism and Prophecy in Ancient Israel and the Near East*. JSOT Supplement Series. Sheffield, UK: Sheffield Academic Press Ltd., 2001.

Gray, John. *I & II Kings: A Commentary*, Old Testament Library. Philadelphia: Westminster, 1963.

Greenblatt, Stephen. *Learning to Curse: Essays in Early Modern Culture*. New York: Routledge, 1990.

———. *Renaissance Self-Fashioning: From More to Shakespeare*. Chicago: University of Chicago Press, 1980.

———. *Shakespearean Negotiations: The Circulation of Social Energy in Renaissance England*. Berkeley: University of California Press, 1988.

Greenfield, Jonas. *Storia e tradizioni di Israele*. Brescia, Italy: Paideia Editrice, 1991.
Gunkel, Hermann. *Elias, Jahve und Baal*. Religionsgeschichtliche Volksbucher, 2/2. Tubingen, Germany: Mohr, 1906.
Hamilton, Clayton Meeker. *A Manual of the Art of Fiction*. Garden City, NJ: Doubleday, 1918.
Harner, Michael. "The Ecological Basis for Aztec Sacrifice." *American Ethnologist* 4 (1979): 17–35.
Harris, Marvin. *Cannibals and Kings: The Origins of Cultures*. New York: Random House, 1977.
Harvey, William J. *Character and the Novel*. Ithaca, NY: Cornell University Press, 1966.
Haught, Nancy. *Sacred Strangers: What the Bible's Outsiders Can Teach Christians*. Collegeville, MN: Liturgical Press, 2017.
Hens-Piazza, Gina. "Biblical Interpretation as Praxis of Justice: 'Whoever wishes to become great among you must be your servant . . .' (Mark 10:43)." In *Scripture and Social Justice: Catholic Ecumenical Essays*, eds. Anathea A. Portier-Young and Gregory A. Sterling. Lanham, MD: Lexington Books/Fortress Press, 2017, 107–24.
———. "Forms of Violence and the Violence of Forms: Two Cannibal Mothers before a King (2 Kings 6:24-33." *Journal of Feminist Studies in Religion* 14 (1998): 91–104.
———. *Lamentations: Wisdom Commentary*, vol. 30. Collegeville, MN: Liturgical Press, 2017.
———. "Lyotard." In *Handbook of Postmodern Biblical Interpretation*, edited by A. K. M. Adam. St. Louis, MO: Chalice Press, 2000.
———. *The New Historicism*, Guides to Biblical Scholarship. Minneapolis: Fortress Press, 2001.
———. *Of Methods, Monarchs, and Meanings: A Socio-Rhetorical Approach to Exegesis*. Macon, GA: Macon Press, 1996.
———. *1–2 Kings*, Abingdon Old Testament Commentaries. Nashville: Abingdon Press, 2006.
Hobbs, T. R. *2 Kings Word Book Commentary*. Waco, TX: Word Publishers, 1985.
Hochman, Baruch. *Character in Literature*. Ithaca, NY: Cornell University Press, 1985.
Holland, Norman N. *The Dynamics of Literary Response*. New York: W. W. Norton, 1975.
hooks, bell. "Keepers of Hope." *Teaching Community: A Pedagogy of Hope*. New York: Routledge Press, 2003.
Hoover, Tamaris Renteria. "The Elijah/Elisha Stories: A Sociocultural Analysis of Prophets and People in Ninth-Century B.C.E. Israel." *Elisha and Elisha in Socioliterary Perspective*, edited by Robert Coote. Atlanta, GA: Scholars Press, 1992.
House, Paul R. *1, 2 Kings. The New American Commentary*. Nashville: Broadman & Holman Publishers, 1995.
Hutcheon, Linda. *The Poetics of Postmodernism: History, Theory, Fiction*. New York: Routledge, 1988.
Ingarden, Roman. *The Literary Work of Art: An Investigation on the Borderlines of Ontology, Logic, and Theory of Literature*. Translated by George C. Grabowicz. Evanston, IL: Northwestern University Press, 1973.
Iser, Wolfgang. *The Act of Reading: A Theory of Aesthetic Response*. Baltimore, MD: Johns Hopkins University Press, 1978.
———. "The Reading Process: A Phenomenological Approach." In *Reader-Response Criticism: From Formalism to Post-Structuralism*, edited by Jane P. Tompkins. Baltimore, MD: Johns Hopkins University Press, 1980).
James, Henry. "The Art of Fiction." In *Art of Fiction and Other Essays by Henry James*, edited by Morris Roberts. New York: Oxford University Press, 1948, originally published 1884.
Jones, G. H. *1 and 2 Kings*, vol. 2. The New Century Bible Commentary. Grand Rapids, MI: William B. Eerdmans, 1984.
Kang, Jung Ju. *The Persuasive Portrayal of Solomon in I Kings 1–11*. Bern, Switzerland: Peter Lang, 2003.
Kierkegaard, Soren. *Soren Kierkegaard's Journals and Papers*, vol. 4. Translated by Howard V. Hong and Edna H. Hong. Bloomington: Indiana University Press, 1975.
Kim, Jean Kyoung. "Reading and Retelling Naaman's Story (2 Kings 5)." *Journal for the Study of the Old Testament*, 30 (2005): 49–61.

Kuan, Jeffrey. "Third Kingdoms 5.1 and Israelite-Tyrian Relations during the Reign of Solomon." *Journal for the Study of the Old Testament* 46 (1990): 39.

LaBarbera, Robert. "The Man of War and the Man of God: Social Satire in 2 Kings 6:8–7:20." *Catholic Biblical Quarterly* 46 (1984): 646–47.

Lasine, Stuart. "Jehoram and the Cannibal Mothers (2 Kings 6.24–33): Solomon's Judgment in an Inverted World." *Journal for the Study of the Old Testament* 50 (1991): 48.

Latvus, Kari. "Debt and Interest in the Hebrew Bible: The Silently Indebted in Ancient Israel and Their Finnish Companions Today." In *Exodus and Deuteronomy*, edited by Athalya Brenner and Gale A. Yee. Minneapolis: Fortress Press, 2012.

Linafelt, Tod. *The Book of Ruth*. Berit Olam: Studies in Hebrew Narrative & Poetry. Collegeville, MN: Liturgical Press, 1999.

Long, Burke. *1 Kings:* The Forms of the Old Testament Literature. Grand Rapids, MI: Wm. B. Eerdmans Publishing Co., 1984.

———. *2 Kings : Forms of the Old Testament Literature,* vol X. Grand Rapids, MI: William B. Eerdmans Publishing Company, 1991.

Lubbock, Percy. *The Craft of Fiction*. New York: The Viking Press, 1957.

Lyotard, Jean-Francois. "Lessons in Pragmatis." Translated by David Macey in *The Lyotard Reader,* edited by Andrew Benjamin. Oxford and Cambridge: Basil Blackwell, 1989.

———. *The Postmodern Condition*. Translated by Geoff Bennington and Brian Massumi. Theory and History of Literature 10. Minneapolis: University of Minnesota Press, 1984.

McKenzie, Steven. *1 Kings 16–2 Kings 16*. International Exegetical Commentary on the Old Testament. Stuttgart, Germany: W. Kohlhammer, 2019.

Menn, Esther M. "A Little Child Shall Lead Them: The Role of the Little Israelite Servant Girl (2 Kings 5. 1–19)." *Currents in Theology and Mission* 35 (October 2008): 343.

Montgomery, James, and Henry Gehman. *The Books of Kings,* International Critical Commentary. New York: Scribner's, 1957.

Moore, Rick Dale. *God Saves: Lessons from the Elisha Stories*. Sheffield: Sheffield Academic Press, 1990.

Moore, Stephen, ed. *Biblical Studies and the New Historicism* (thematic issue), *Biblical Interpretation* 5, no. 4, 1997.

Mulder, Martin. *1 Kings: Volume 1: 1 Kings 1–11*. Leuven, Belgium: Peeters, 1998.

Nelson, Richard. *First and Second Kings,* Interpretation Commentary. Atlanta, GA: John Knox, 1987.

Newsom, Carol A., Sharon H. Ringe, and Jacqueline E. Lapsley, eds. *Women's Bible Commentary*, 3rd edition, Revised and Updated. Louisville, KY: Westminster John Knox Press, 2012.

O'Connor, Michael Patrick. "The Biblical Notion of the City." In *Constructions of Space II: The Biblical City and Other Imagined Spaces,* edited by John Berquist and Claudia Camp. New York: T&T Clark Library of Biblical Studies, 2008.

Olowin, Mary. "The Pathos of Choice," in *Lamentations: Wisdom Commentary*, 66–67.

Overholt, Thomas. *Channels of Prophecy: The Social Dynamics of Prophetic Activity*. Minneapolis: Fortress Press, 1989.

Prince, Gerald. "Introduction to the Study of the Narratee." In *Reader-Response Criticism: From Formalism to Post-Structuralism,* ed. Jane P. Tompkins. Baltimore, MD: Johns Hopkins University Press, 1980.

Provan, Iain. *1 and 2 Kings,* New International Biblical Commentary. Peabody, MA: Hendrickson Publishers, 1995.

Pyper, Hugh. "Judging the Wisdom of Solomon: The Two-Way Effect of Intertextuality." *Journal of the Study of the Old Testament 59* (1993): 34.

Robinson, J. *The First Book of Kings*. London: Cambridge University Press, 1972.

Rosen, Jeremy. *Minor Characters Have Their Day: Genre and the Contemporary Literary Marketplace*. New York: Columbia University Press, 2016.

Sahlins, Marshall. "Culture as Protein and Profit." *New York Review of Books,* 25 (1978): 45–53.

Sanday, Peggy Reeves. *Divine Hunger: Cannibalism as a Cultural System*. Cambridge, UK: Cambridge University Press, 1986.

Schottroff, Luise, and Marie-Theres Wacker, eds. *Feminist Biblical Interpretation: A Compendium of Critical Commentary on the Books of the Bible and Related Literature.* Grand Rapids, MI: Eerdmans, 2012.

Schwartz, Regina. *The Curse of Cain: The Violent Legacy of Monotheism.* Chicago: The University of Chicago Press, 1997.

Seibert, Eric. *Subversive Scribes and the Solomonic Narrative: A Rereading of I Kings 1–11.* New York: T&T Clark Library of Biblical Studies, 2003.

Shemesh, Yael. "Elisha and the Miraculous Jug of Oil." *The Journal of Hebrew Scriptures*, vol. 8, no. 4 (2008): 9.

Smagorinsky, Peter. "If Meaning Is Constructed, What Is It Made From? Toward a Cultural Theory of Reading." *Review of Educational Research* 71, no. 1 (2001): 133–69.

Sugirtharajah, R. S. *The Postcolonial Biblical Reader.* Hoboken, NJ: Wiley-Blackwell, 2005.

Telford, Kenneth A. *Aristotle's Poetics.* Translated by Kenneth A. Telford. Chicago: Regnery, 1961.

Thompson, Henry O. "Jordan River." *Anchor Bible Dictionary*, vol. 3, edited by David Noel Freedman. New York: Doubleday, 1992.

Tierney, R. J., and P. D. Pearson. "Towards a Composing Model of Reading." *Language Arts* 60 (1983): 568–80.

Todorov, Tzyetan. *Qu'est-ce c' est la structuralisme.* Paris: Editions du Seuil, 1973.

———. "Reading as Construction." In *The Reader in the Text: Essays on Audience Interpretation*, edited by Susan R. Suleiman and Inge Crosman. Princeton, NJ: Princeton University Press, 1980.

Tompkins, Jane, ed. *Reader Response Criticism: From Formalism to Post-Structuralism.* Baltimore, MD: Johns Hopkins University Press, 1980.

Trible, Phyllis. *God and the Rhetoric of Sexuality,* Overtures to Biblical Theology. Philadelphia: Fortress Press, 1978.

von Rad, Gerhard. "Naaman: A Critical Retelling." In *God at Work in Israel.* Translated by J. H. Mark. Nashville: Abingdon Press, 1980.

Walsh, Jerome. *I Kings.* Berit Olam: Studies in Hebrew Narrative & Poetry. Collegeville, MN: Liturgical Press, 1996.

Wellek, Rene, and Austin Warren. *Theory of Literature.* London: Cape Publishers, 1966.

Wertsch, J. *Voices of the Mind: A Sociocultural Approach to Mediated Action.* Cambridge, MA: Harvard University Press, 1993.

Wilson, Robert. *Prophecy and Society in Ancient Israel.* Philadelphia: Fortress Press, 1980.

Woloch, Alex. *The One vs. the Many: Minor Characters and the Space of the Protagonist in the Novel.* Princeton, NJ: Princeton University Press, 2003.

Wright, David, and Richard Jones. "Leprosy." *Anchor Bible Dictionary*, vol. 4, edited by David Noel Freedman. New York: Doubleday, 1992.

Scripture Index

Genesis 38:28–29, 6
Genesis 45:22, 64n20

Exodus 2:15, 22
Exodus 2:15b–22, 22
Exodus 2:21–22, 23
Exodus 10:2, 35–36
Exodus 12:26, 35–36
Exodus 13:8, 35–36
Exodus 20:16–17, 74
Exodus 21:7, 70
Exodus 21:14, 74
Exodus 21:18, 74
Exodus 21:35, 74
Exodus 22:7–11, 74
Exodus 22:14, 74
Exodus 22:21, 73
Exodus 22:21–24, 72
Exodus 22:22, 73
Exodus 22:24–26, 73
Exodus 22:26, 74
Exodus 32:27, 74
Exodus 33:11, 74
Exodus 34:6, 40
Exodus 35:10f, 6

Leviticus 13–14, 63n4
Leviticus 13:44–46, 64n21
Leviticus 19:18, 74
Leviticus 25, 70
Leviticus 25:35–38, 71

Numbers 35:5, 86

Deuteronomy 4:9, 35–36
Deuteronomy 4:31, 40
Deuteronomy 6:7, 35–36
Deuteronomy 6:20–25, 35–36
Deuteronomy 10:18, 72
Deuteronomy 14:28–29, 72
Deuteronomy 15:1–18, 70
Deuteronomy 17:7, 83
Deuteronomy 24:17, 72, 73
Deuteronomy 24:19, 72, 73
Deuteronomy 24:22, 72
Deuteronomy 27:19, 72
Deuteronomy 28:53–57, 35, 38
Deuteronomy 28:56–57, 37
Deuteronomy 32:7, 35–36
Deuteronomy 32:46, 35–36

Joshua 7:16–18, 92n21
Joshua 11:21–23, 6
Joshua 19:27, 84
Joshua 20:7, 84

Judges 11:39, 8
Judges 14:12, 64n20
Judges 16:1–3, 6
Judges 21:15–24, 6

Ruth 1:1–8, 72
Ruth 1:16–17, 72

Ruth 1:20, 72
Ruth 2:2–23, 28–29
Ruth 2:3, 28–29
Ruth 4:9–10, 86

1 Samuel 16:14–17, 5
2 Samuel 11:2, 15, 17–18
2 Samuel 11:5, 17
2 Samuel 11:6–21, 17
2 Samuel 14:1–24, 25

1 Kings 3–8, 81
1 Kings 3:13, 84
1 Kings 3:15–28, 46n23
1 Kings 4:7–19, 87
1 Kings 5–8, 80
1 Kings 5:12–18, 80, 82–83
1 Kings 6:38, 82
1 Kings 7:1, 82
1 Kings 7:13–14, 82–83
1 Kings 9, 81
1 Kings 9:10, 81, 82
1 Kings 9:10–11, 8
1 Kings 9:10–14, 80–81, 81, 90
1 Kings 9:11, 81, 82–83
1 Kings 9:11b, 84, 85
1 Kings 9:11–13, 88
1 Kings 9:12, 81, 84
1 Kings 9:13, 81, 84, 84–85
1 Kings 9:14, 83
1 Kings 9:15–21, 95
1 Kings 9:20–21, 6
1 Kings 9:28, 83
1 Kings 10:2, 83
1 Kings 10:14, 83
1 Kings 10:22, 83
1 Kings 10:23, 84
1 Kings 12:6–7, 95
1 Kings 21, 71, 88
1 Kings 21:27, 41

2 Kings 1:13–16, 6–7
2 Kings 2:13–14, 95
2 Kings 2:19–22, 55
2 Kings 3:10, 64n26
2 Kings 3:13–14, 55
2 Kings 4:1, 27, 68, 70, 72, 73
2 Kings 4:1–4, 68
2 Kings 4:1–7, 8, 27, 55, 67–68, 95, 96

2 Kings 4:2, 68
2 Kings 4:3, 74, 75, 76
2 Kings 4:3–4, 68
2 Kings 4:4, 75
2 Kings 4:5, 27, 68
2 Kings 4:5–6, 68
2 Kings 4:6, 27, 68, 69, 72
2 Kings 4:7, 27, 68
2 Kings 4:8–37, 67
2 Kings 4:18–37, 55
2 Kings 4:38–41, 55, 67
2 Kings 4:42–44, 6, 55, 67
2 Kings 5:1, 49, 50, 52
2 Kings 5:1–14, 48, 49, 50
2 Kings 5:1–19, 93, 97
2 Kings 5:2, 50, 51, 52, 56
2 Kings 5:2–3, 9, 49, 50
2 Kings 5:2–4, 50
2 Kings 5:3, 51–52, 53
2 Kings 5:4, 50
2 Kings 5:5, 53
2 Kings 5:6, 53
2 Kings 5:7, 55
2 Kings 5:9, 57
2 Kings 5:10, 57
2 Kings 5:11, 58
2 Kings 5:12, 58, 58–59
2 Kings 5:13, 50, 59–60, 60
2 Kings 5:13–14, 9
2 Kings 5:14, 56
2 Kings 5:15, 49, 61–62
2 Kings 5:15–19, 48, 49, 61
2 Kings 5:17a, 62
2 Kings 5:17b, 62
2 Kings 5:18a, 62
2 Kings 5:18b, 62
2 Kings 5:20–27, 48, 49
2 Kings 6:1–7, 55
2 Kings 6:2–3, 55
2 Kings 6:8–7:20, 34
2 Kings 6:21–23, 34
2 Kings 6:23–31, 5–6, 93
2 Kings 6:24, 34, 36, 55
2 Kings 6:24–33, 34, 42, 46n23
2 Kings 6:26, 34, 40, 44n3
2 Kings 6:27, 34, 44n3
2 Kings 6:28–29, 34
2 Kings 6:30, 35
2 Kings 6:31, 35, 42, 64n26

2 Kings 6:32, 35, 95
2 Kings 6:33, 35, 45n4
2 Kings 7:1–2, 34
2 Kings 7:3–11, 6
2 Kings 11:1–3, 7
2 Kings 11:2–3, 95
2 Kings 23, 30
2 Kings 23:7, 8

2 Chronicles 26:16–21, 64n21
2 Chronicles 30:9, 40

Nehemiah 5:3–5, 70
Nehemiah 9:17, 40
Nehemiah 9:31, 40

Psalms 78:38, 40
Psalms 86:1, 40
Psalms 103:8, 40
Psalms 111:4, 40
Psalms 145:8, 40

Proverbs 1:8, 35
Proverbs 6:20, 35
Proverbs 30:8, 83

Isaiah 3:5, 74
Isaiah 8:23, 84
Isaiah 50:1, 70

Jeremiah 9:4–9, 74

Lamentations 2:20, 37
Lamentations 4:1, 40
Lamentations 4:4, 40
Lamentations 4:8, 40
Lamentations 4:9, 40
Lamentations 4:10, 37, 40

Ezekiel 5:10, 37

Hosea 4:2, 71
Hosea 5:10, 71
Hosea 12:7–8, 71

Joel 2:13, 40

Amos 2:6, 70
Amos 2:6–8, 71
Amos 5:8–12, 71
Amos 5:11a, 8
Amos 8:6, 70

Jonah 3:5, 41
Jonah 3:8–9, 41
Jonah 4:2, 40

Micah 2:9, 70
Micah 7:5–6, 74

Hebrews 8–9, 71

Romans 11:1, 87

Subject Index

Abana (river), 58, 59
Abrams, M. H., 23
Absalom, 25–26
action: of bit-part characters, 47–48, 56; of complementary characters, 25, 33, 34; hierarchy of characters and, 4, 5; in literary studies, primacy of, 13. *See also* dialogue
agents, 23–24, 50. *See also* characters
Ahab (king), 71, 88
Alter, Robert, 5
ancestry, 87, 88, 89
antagonists, 4, 5. *See also* characters; protagonists
anthropology, 38. *See also* famine
apostasy, 36, 88
Aram: and Israel, conflict with, 34, 36, 41, 42, 49; and Israel, victory over, 48–49, 50; Naaman's allegiance to, 48, 52–53, 58; rivers in, 58, 59; skin diseases, acceptance of, 54
Aram's king, 48, 49, 52–53, 53. *See also* Naaman
Aristotle, 13
"The Art of Fiction" (James), 13
Asherah, 8, 30
Auerbach, Eric, 6
authority, language of, 57. *See also* Elisha
authors: character hierarchy, influence on, 19, 95–96; implied readers and, 79; narrators vs., 22; vision of, respecting, 8

awareness, alternative readings and increased: of displaced peoples, 88–89, 90–91; of multiplicity of stories, 8, 21, 24, 30, 65; of power and marginalization, 3, 11, 30, 50, 62–63; of real-world heroes, 9–10, 21, 56, 62, 96, 97; of self, 10; of systematic violence, 43, 44, 96–97; of unrecognized contributions to society, 26, 28, 29, 77

Bakhtin, Michel, 4
Barthes, Roland, 7
Bathsheba, 15, 17–18, 54
Ben-Hadad (Aramean king), 34, 36, 41, 42
Benjamin, tribe of, 86–87
Berlin, Adele, 23
Bible: alternative readings of, 11, 16–17, 30, 50, 97–98; bit-part characters in, 47–48; cannibalism in, 37–38, 39–40; as cultural force, 1; hierarchy of values in, 8; implied readers of, 79; narrative style of, 4–5; narrator of, 35; world interpretation and, 3, 9–10, 20, 21, 96. *See also* Bible, historical context of; biblical studies
Bible, historical context of: cities, size of, 86; debt slavery, 71–73; goods, value of, 36–37, 53; kinship, in ancient Israel, 74–75, 86–87; motherhood, in ancient Israel, 35–36; widowhood, in ancient

Israel, 36
biblical studies: alternative readings in, 11, 16–17, 21, 30, 97–98; character categories in, 23–24; feminism and, 19, 94; mimesis in, 20; postcolonial theory and, 94; prophets and kings, focus on, 94–95. *See also* Bible; Bible, historical context of; literary studies
bit parts, 24; and complementary characters, compared, 48; definition of, 26–27, 47; fluid classification of, 93; in Naaman's story, 49–50; significance of, 47–48. *See also* children, of widowed woman; servant girl; servants of Naaman
Boaz, 28–29, 86
Booth, Wayne, 6
building projects, 71, 80–81, 82, 82–83

Cabul, 81, 84, 85, 90. *See also* Galilee, inhabitants of
cameo appearances, 24; brotherhood of prophets, 69; the creditor, 70–74; definition of, 28, 66; dialogue, absence of, 76; fluid classification of, 93; initial impressions of, 65–66; in Naaman's story, 49; the neighbors, 74–77; reapers of Boaz, 28–29; significance of, 65–67, 95; strategies for studying, 67
cannibalism: in biblical tradition, 37–38, 39–40; compassion of, 40, 44; cultural domination and, 38–39, 44, 45n18; as cultural practice, 38; curse of disobedience and, 38; famine as source of, 37–38, 38–39; poverty and, 37. *See also* cannibal mother of Samaria
cannibal mother of Samaria: agency of, 35–36, 42; categorization of, 93; and Israel's king, compared, 40–41, 42; lessons from story of, 35, 43, 44; marginalization of, 37, 41–42, 42–43; and mothers of Jerusalem, compared, 39–40; narrative space of, 37, 42–43; physical appearance of, 40; plea to Israel's king, 34, 37, 40–42; plot, influence on, 35, 39; social and political context of, 36, 37, 41; as victim of violence, 37–38, 39, 44, 97. *See also* complementary roles

capital, human settlements as, 84–85, 86, 87–90
cast, supporting. *See* supporting cast
caste system, narrative: biblical, 8; character classification, 3, 3–4, 23–24, 49–50; characters, naming of, 7–8, 9, 22; chiastic framework and, 42–43; emancipation from, 8–9, 21, 30, 62, 90, 97–98; narratives, grand vs. little, 18–19; narrators, influence of, 21–22; reader responsibility and, 8, 9–10, 11, 30, 43. *See also* space, narrative
centrality, challenges to, 94–96. *See also* awareness, alternative readings and increased
character development, reader participation in: bit parts, 48; cameo characters, 67; implied characters, 29–30, 80; interpretation process and, 13–14, 18; interpretation processes and, 15, 15–16, 19; projection, 9; responsibility for, 10, 24. *See also* characters
characterization: discordant, 85; naming and, 7, 22; narrator authority in, 21–22; nomenclature of, 4, 6, 19–20, 24, 80. *See also* character development, reader participation in
characters: classification of, 4, 6, 23–24; definitions of, 13–15, 18, 23–24; Hens-Piazza's categories of, 24; labor theory of, 19–20, 50; major, centrality of, 3, 94; minor, challenge to term, 11, 19–20, 25–26, 93–94; naming, importance of, 7, 9, 22; narrative analysis and, 13; narrators and, 22; reception theory and, 4, 9, 15. *See also* character development, reader participation in; characters, biblical; space, narrative; supporting cast; *specific characters*
characters, biblical: characterization of, vivid, 15–16; cultural significance of, 2; naming, politics of, 7, 9; rudimentary nature of, 4–6, 16. *See also* characters; reading practices, alternative; supporting cast; *specific characters*
character studies. *See* literary studies
Chatman, Seymour, 4, 6
chiastic framework, 42–43
children, in Israelite society, 35–36, 40

Subject Index

children, of widowed woman: as payment for debt, 70, 71–73, 96; significance of, 69, 95; story summary of, 27, 68. *See also* bit parts
choice, pathos of, 43–44
cities. *See* settlements, human
classism: cannibalism and, 39; challenges to, 25–26, 56, 62; labor theory of character, 19–20, 50; narrative hierarchy and, 3, 9, 21, 37; prophet condemnation of, 36. *See also* wealth
community. *See* kinship; neighbors
compassion, of cannibalism, 40, 44
complementary roles, 24; and bit parts, compared, 48; definition of, 25; fluid classification of, 93; influence of, 25, 33–34; wise woman of Tekoa, 25–26. *See also* cannibal mother of Samaria; widowed woman
conversion, 48–49, 56, 61–62, 93. *See also* Naaman
Covenant Code, 73, 74. *See also* Bible, historical context of; laws, Israelite
the creditor: character of, moral, 71–72, 73–74, 76–77, 96; historical context of, 73; legal legitimacy of, 70, 72, 73, 77, 96; significance of, 70, 77, 95; story summary of, 68–69. *See also* cameo appearances
Culler, Jonathan, 95
cultural systems, 38–39. *See also* cannibalism
curse of disobedience, 35, 38

Damascus, 58, 59
David (king), 5, 15, 17–18, 25–26, 54
debt: children as payment for, 8, 27, 68, 69; creditors and, 70, 71; poverty and, 70–71; slavery, legality of, 70, 71, 73, 96. *See also* widowed woman
de Certeau, Michel, 9
democratization of reading. *See* reading, alternative practices of
destiny, 28, 39, 44, 69
development, character. *See* character development, reader participation in
dialogue: of bit-part characters, 26–27, 47–48; of cameo characters, 28, 65, 76, 95; of cannibal mother of Samaria, 41–42; character development and, 4, 5, 7, 13–15; of complementary characters, 25, 33, 34, 37; of Hiram, 81, 84; of kings and citizens, 41–42; of Naaman, 57–59; of servant girl of Naaman, 51–52; of servants of Naaman, 50, 59–60, 60–61; of supporting cast, 5, 9, 17, 93; of widowed woman and children, 68, 69. *See also* action
discourse, narrated vs. direct, 47–48. *See also* dialogue
disobedience, curse of, 35, 38
distributional matrix, of characters, 19, 80. *See also* characters
divine intervention. *See* Elisha
domestic sphere, 35–36, 39
domination, cultural, 38–39, 45n18. *See also* hierarchy; power

Elisha: divine intermediation of, 54–55; Jehoram and, 5–6, 42, 43, 55, 57; Naaman, healing of, 9, 48–49, 51–53, 56, 57–58; as prophet of common people, 54–55, 67–68; Samarian famine and, 34, 35, 42; servant girl's faith in, 52, 53, 54, 55. *See also* widowed woman
empathy, of readers, 17–18. *See also* awareness, alternative readings and increased
ethic of care, 76–77. *See also* neighbors
exploitation, 8, 19–20, 36, 71

family. *See* kinship
famine: cannibalism and, 37–38, 38–39; food sources and economy of, 36–37; in Jerusalem, 39–40; in Samaria, 34–35, 39, 41; war as cause of, 43–44; widowhood in, 36. *See also* cannibal mother of Samaria
fasting, 41
feminism, 19, 24, 94
Fish, Stanley, 29
folk wisdom, 26
food stress. *See* famine
Forster, E. M., 4, 5, 23

Galef, David, 19

Galilee, inhabitants of: geographic history and, 84; identity of, 86; implied presence of, 7–8, 85; settlements of, as capital, 81, 81–82, 82, 84, 84–85; trade, impact on, 82, 86, 87–89, 90. *See also* implied characters
Gass, William, 7
Gehazi (Elisha's servant), 48, 49
gold, 80, 83–84. *See also* Solomon
grand narratives, 18–19. *See also* literary studies
greatness, meaning of, 60. *See also* heroism

Hamilton, Clayton, 4
harmony, cultural, 38, 45n17. *See also* cannibalism
Harvey, William, 6
healing of Naaman: conditions of, 51–53; Elisha's, 49, 56; instructions for, 57–58; Naaman's wife and, 49; risk involved in, 54; servant girl's role in, 9, 49–50, 50–51, 55, 93; servants' role in, 59–60, 61, 93
heroism: artifice of, 21, 62; of Naaman's servants, 56, 62; supporting cast and real-life, 9–10, 21, 96, 97
hierarchy: breakdown of, 25–26, 56, 62; cannibalism and, 38–39; creditor as symbol of, 77; in Israelite society, 36, 37, 41, 73–74
hierarchy, narrative. *See* caste system, narrative
Hiram: moral character of, 85; and Solomon, conflict with, 81, 82, 84–85; and Solomon, trade with, 80–82, 82, 82–83, 86, 90
Hochman, Baruch, 4, 18
Holland, Norman, 4, 9
homeplace, 86–87, 88–89. *See also* kinship
hooks, bell, 76
hope, 52, 72, 76, 77
hunger. *See* famine
Hutchinson, Linda, 20

identity: of children, mothers and, 36; community, 76, 82; of Galilee inhabitants, 86; kinship and, 87–88; land and, 88–89, 90; war and, 43–44. *See also* self, theory of
implied characters, 24; definition of, 29, 79–80; fluid classification of, 93; narrative space of, 80; readers, dependency on, 29–30, 80, 90; strategies for studying, 82; value of studying, 90–91. *See also* Galilee, inhabitants of
inclusivity: in Naaman's story, 49, 56, 64n27; in reading practices, 3, 19–21, 24–25, 74, 90–91, 97–98. *See also* awareness, alternative readings and increased
Ingarden, Roman, 15
interpretation: character classification and, 5–6, 20, 21; feminist, 19, 24; mimesis and, 20; of narrators, 22; reader's role in, 15, 15–17; textual and real-world, relationship of, 3, 20; textual limitations on, 18. *See also* reading practices, alternative
introjection, 9. *See also* character development, reader participation in; reception theory
Iser, Wolfgang, 4, 9, 15, 79
Israel: cannibalism in, 37–38; community care in, 72, 73, 74–75, 76–77; creditors in, 70, 71; economic pressures in, 71; famine in, 34–35, 36, 39–40; healing in, 52–53; kinship and homeplace in, 86–87, 88, 89; monarchic hierarchy in, 36; motherhood in, 35–36; Naaman's victory over, 48–49, 50; pastoral society in, 86, 87, 88; as Phoenicia's granary, 83; reapers of Boaz and, 29; Samaria vs., 54; skin diseases in, 54; widowhood in, 36, 72–73. *See also* Galilee, inhabitants of
Israel's king. *See* Jehoram

James, Henry, 13
Jehoram (king): cannibal mother and, 34–35, 37, 40–42, 42–43; Elisha and, 42, 43, 55, 57; Naaman and, 49, 53; and servant girl, compared, 55–56
Jerusalem: Babylonian siege on, 39–40; size of, 86; Solomon's projects in, 80–81

Jesus, 49
Joab, 25
Jordan River, 9, 57, 58, 60
Josiah, 8, 30

Kierkegaard, Soren, 4
kinship: in cities, 82; definition and importance of, 87; disruption of, in Israel, 71, 75, 77, 87–88, 88–89; homeplace vs., 86–87, 88; as identity in Israel, 86; of Naaman and servants, 62

labor theory of character, 19–20, 50. *See also* caste system, narrative
land, importance and ownership of, 71, 87, 88–89. *See also* Galilee, inhabitants of
language, power and limitation of, 9
laws, Israelite: debt, protection from, 70, 71, 73; on debt slavery, 70, 73; kinship and, 74–75
literary studies: caste system in, 21–22; character analysis in, 13, 19–20, 85, 94; minor characters, recasting of, 16; New Historicism, 20, 94; postmodernism, influence of, 18–19, 94. *See also* biblical studies; caste system, narrative; character development, reader participation in; characters
loans, 70–71, 73. *See also* debt
location, narrative. *See* space, narrative
Lubbock, Percy, 6
Lyotard, Jean-Francois, 18

major characters. *See* characters
marginalization: of cannibal mother of Samaria, 37, 41–42, 42–43; of Naaman, 54; of servants of Naaman, 50, 54; of supporting cast, 94–96; of widowed woman, 76. *See also* caste system, narrative
Marx, Karl, 7, 19
materialism, 38
meaning, multiplicity of, 6
memory, 9, 33. *See also* supporting cast
migrants, 88–89
mimesis, 20
minor characters. *See* characters; supporting cast
miracles. *See* Elisha

monarchy: and citizens, dialogue of, 41–42; conflict and, 35, 42, 43, 55, 97; power and Israelite, 36, 39, 41, 42, 85; rejection of Israel's, 75; scholarly focus on, 94–95; subjugation and, 17; tribal relations and, 87–88. *See also* Galilee, inhabitants of; kinship; *specific monarchs*
morality, 1, 44, 76, 96
Moses, 6, 22–23
motherhood: in Israelite society, 35–36, 37; war and failed, 40, 43–44. *See also* cannibal mother of Samaria; widowed woman
multiplicity of meanings, 6, 21. *See also* reading practices, alternative

Naaman (Syrian general): background on, 48, 49; conversion of, 48–49, 56, 61–62, 93; Elisha's orders to, 57–58; healing, responsibility of, 51–52; healing, risk of seeking, 54; and his servants, compared, 60–61; nationalism and egotism of, 53, 55, 57, 57–59; and servant girl, compared, 51, 53, 56, 62; servant girl, disregard of, 52–53, 53; servant girl, influence of, 49–50, 50–51, 56, 61–62, 93; servants, influence of, 49–50, 59–60, 61, 62; wife of, 9, 49, 51
Naboth, 88
naming: of bit-part characters, 48, 51, 61; of cameo characters, 28, 66; of complementary characters, 25, 33; narrative hierarchy and character, 7, 9, 22
Naomi, 29, 72
narrative: archaeology of, 28; biblical, distinctiveness of, 4–5; characters and analysis of, 13; chiastic framework in, 42–43; reader expansion of, 30. *See also* caste system, narrative; characters; literary studies; space, narrative
narrative studies. *See* literary studies
narrators: authority of, 21–22, 22–23, 57, 97; biblical, theological purpose of, 35; as characters, 22; definition of, 22; supporting cast and, 25, 47–48, 80
neighbors: meaning and history of, 74–75; social transformation and, 76; widowed

woman, assistance to, 75–76, 77, 95, 96. *See also* cameo appearances; kinship

New Historicism, 20, 94. *See also* literary studies

Omride dynasty, 54, 55, 71, 73. *See also* Israel

The One vs. the Many (Woloch), 19

ontology, 10. *See also* reading practices, alternative

otherness: of cannibal mother of Samaria, 39; of Galilee inhabitants in Tyre, 89; reader recognition of, 10–11, 44; self, theory of and, 4, 10; skin diseases and, 54. *See also* awareness, alternative readings and increased; marginalization

Palestine, 86

paradigm of traits, 4. *See also* caste system, narrative; characters

patriarchy, 19, 72, 87

Paul, 87

Pharpar (river), 58, 59

Phoenicia, 80, 83

plot: bit-part characters and, 47–48; cannibal mother of Samaria and, 35, 39; complementary characters and, 25, 33, 34; servants of Naaman and, 53, 61; widowed woman and, 68–69. *See also* dialogue; subplots

The Poetics of Postmodernism (Hutchinson), 20

point of view, 19, 95. *See also* character development, reader participation in

postcolonial theory, 94

postmodernism, 18–19, 94

poverty: in ancient cities, 37; of citizens, monarchy and, 36; debt and, 70–71, 73; widowhood and, 72. *See also* wealth; widowed woman

power: authorities in struggle for, 35, 42–43, 55, 97; of Bible, cultural, 1; of Elisha, 55, 67–68; of Israelite monarchs, 36, 39, 41, 42, 85; landless migrants and international, 88–89, 90; of narrators, 21–22, 22–23, 57, 93. *See also* caste system, narrative; wealth

Prince, Gerald, 79

privilege. *See* caste system, narrative; power; wealth

projection, 9, 18. *See also* character development, reader participation in

prophets: as divine intermediaries, 54–55; and kings, conflict of, 35, 36, 42, 43, 97; on peasants, vulnerability of, 71; scholarly focus on, 94–95. *See also* Elisha

protagonists: bit-part characters and, 47; cameo appearances and, 66; character classification and, 4, 6, 19; complementary characters and, 33, 33–34; reader's elaboration of, 16; shifting focus from, 3, 10, 21, 94; supporting casts' enhancement of, 2, 6–8. *See also* characters; supporting cast

reader response theory: explanation of, 15; implied vs. real readers, 79; postmodernism and, 19, 94; reception and production in, 4, 9–10, 94; textual limitations on, 18. *See also* character development, reader participation in

readers: biblical characters as inspiration for, 2; empathy with characters, 17–18, 96–98; implied vs. real, 79; memory, character influence on, 9, 33; narrator authority and, 22, 23; point of view of, 19, 95; postmodern validation of, 19. *See also* character development, reader participation in; reader response theory; reading practices, alternative

"Reading as Poaching" (de Certeau), 9

reading practices, alternative: Hens-Piazza's promotion of, 2–3, 11, 16–17, 21, 50, 62–63; implied characters and, 90; reader responsibility in, 8, 9–10, 30, 44, 97–98; resistance to narrators, 23

reapers of Boaz, 28–29

reception theory, 4, 9, 94. *See also* character development, reader participation in; reader also response theory

refugees, 88–89. *See also* Galilee, inhabitants of; kinship

representation, 20. *See also* character development, reader participation in;

interpretation
responsibility of readers. *See* reading practices, alternative
Reuel (Midian priest), 22–23
Rosen, Jeremy, 16
Ruth, 28–29, 72, 86

sackcloth, 35, 41
Samaria: famine in, 34–35, 36–37, 39, 44; geographic history of, 54; and Jerusalem famine, compared, 39–40; monarchic power in, 36, 42; Naaman's arrival in, 9, 57. *See also* Israel
self, theory of, 4, 9–10, 20. *See also* identity; literary studies
servant girl: credibility of, 54; faith of, 53, 54, 55–56, 62; idealism of, 52; inclusiveness of, 56; and Jehoram, compared, 55–56; and Naaman, compared, 51, 53, 56, 62; Naaman's disregard of, 52–53, 53; narrative space of, 50, 93; as prisoner of war, 50, 51; rhetorical strategy of, 51–52, 55; significance of, 53, 56, 61–62, 62, 97; value of studying, 49–50. *See also* bit parts
servants of Naaman: and Naaman, compared, 60–61; Naaman's dialogue to, 59; narrative space of, 50, 93; rhetorical strategy of, 59–60, 60–61; significance of, 59, 60–61, 62, 93; value of studying, 49–50. *See also* bit parts
settlements, human: as capital, impact of, 87–90; as capital of monarchs, 81, 82, 84, 84–85; as cultural centers, 82; size and demographics of, biblical, 86; translation of, 85; urban and rural, interdependence of, 86, 87–88
Sheba, Queen of, 83
siege: cannibalism and, 37; of Jerusalem, 39–40; power struggles and, 43; on Samaria, 34, 36, 39, 41–42
skin diseases. *See* Naaman
slavery. *See* debt
sociology of reading, 3. *See also* reading, alternative practices of
Solomon: Bathsheba and, 54; building projects of, 80–81, 82, 95; collective identity, disruption of, 87–89, 90; gold,

affection for, 80, 83–84; and Hiram, conflict with, 81, 82, 84–85; and Hiram, trade with, 80–82, 82, 82–84, 86, 90; moral character of, 82, 85, 90; rejection of monarchy after, 75; slave labor and, 6; two mothers and, 35, 46n23
space, narrative: of bit-part characters, 26–27, 48, 50, 93; of cameo characters, 66; of cannibal mother of Samaria, 37, 42–43; character analysis and, 19, 80; of complementary characters, 33, 34; of implied characters, 80, 90; reader response theory and, 15, 23; of supporting cast, biblical, 4–5, 93, 95–96; of widowed woman, 68
starvation. *See* famine
storytellers. *See* narrators
subaltern, 7, 50
subplots, 34, 35, 48. *See also* bit parts; cannibal mother of Samaria; complementary roles; plot
supporting cast: bit parts, overview, 26–27, 47–48; cameo appearances, overview, 28–29, 65–67; categories of, 24, 93–94; classification of, biblical, 4–5; complementary roles, overview 25–26, 33; definition and function of, 2, 6–8; feminism and, 19, 24, 94; identities of, 5–6, 6–8, 95; implied characters, overview, 29–30, 79–80; lack of attention to, 2, 3–4, 5–6, 10, 23–24; in memory of readers, 9, 33; narrative space of, 5; self-understanding and, 10; significance of, 94–95; strategies for studying, 14, 16–17, 23, 67, 82; value of studying, 8, 10–11, 94–98. *See also* bit parts; cameo appearances; caste system, narrative; character development, reader participation in; complementary roles; dialogue; reading, alternative practices of; space, narrative; *specific characters*
The Supporting Cast (Galef), 19
Syria, 58, 86. *See also* Naaman

Tekoa, 25
Theory of Literature (Wellek), 7
Todorov, Tzvetan, 85

trade: Galilee settlements as capital, 81, 82, 84, 84–85; of gold, Solomon and, 82–84; routes, Omride, 71; of settlements, negative impact of, 82, 86, 87–90; of Solomon and Hiram, duration, 82, 82–83
transgredience, 4. *See also* literary studies
tribal societies: in ancient Israel, 87–88; cannibalism in, 38, 45n18; in Galilee, 84; in northern Israel, 75
truth, literary theories and, 18, 20
types, 23–24, 65. *See also* characters; supporting cast
Tyre, 80–81, 82, 84, 88–89

units of measurement, biblical, 36–37, 53, 83, 86
utilitarianism, 7, 19–20

violence: cannibalism and victims of, 37–38, 39–40, 43–44; of Israel's king, 42; of narrative hierarchy, 9, 21; reader complicity with narrative, 43; recognition of real world, 96. *See also* war

war: cannibalism and, 37, 39–40; dialogue of kings and citizens during, 41–42; famine and, 39–41; impact of, 43–44; of Israel and Aram, 36, 48–49, 50–51, 53; of Israel and Moab, 67. *See also* violence
Warren, Austin, 7
wealth: of creditors, 70, 71, 73; implied characters as symbols of, 66; of Naaman, 53, 57; of Solomon, 82–84. *See also* poverty; power
Wellek, Rene, 7
widowed woman (Elisha and the Oil Jug): agency and significance of, 68–69, 74, 95; children of, 27, 69; creditor and, 70, 72, 73–74, 76–77, 96; debt, origin of, 70–71; Elisha's instructions to, 75, 95; husband of, 69–70, 70–71; legal obligations of, 70, 71, 73; neighbors of, 74, 75–76, 76–77, 95, 96; prospects of, 72, 73–74, 77; story summary of, 8, 27, 68. *See also* complementary roles
wise woman of Tekoa, 25–26
Woloch, Alex, 19–20, 80
women: Bathsheba, 15, 17, 54; characters and feminism, 94; famine, effects on, 37; in Israelite society, 35–36; Naaman's wife, 49, 51; Naomi, 29, 72; in patriarchal society, 72–73; Ruth, 28–29, 72, 86; seven daughters of Reuel, 22–23; wise woman of Tekoa, 25–26; Zipporah, 23; world, creation of, 9, 20. *See also* reader response theory

Zipporah, 23

About the Author

Gina Hens-Piazza is professor of biblical studies in the Joseph S. Alemany Endowed Chair at Santa Clara University's Jesuit School of Theology and professor of biblical studies at the Graduate Theological Union in Berkeley, California. A frequent lecturer nationally and internationally, she is the author of six books, including commentaries on Lamentations and 1 and 2 Kings, and numerous articles addressing topics in literary studies, women's studies, and issues of social justice in the biblical tradition.

www.ingramcontent.com/pod-product-compliance
Lightning Source LLC
Chambersburg PA
CBHW050910300426
44111CB00010B/1466